THE
SHAPE
OF DEATH

THE
SHAPE
OF DEATH

life, death, and immortality
in the early fathers

JAROSLAV PELIKAN

GREENWOOD PRESS, PUBLISHERS
WESTPORT, CONNECTICUT

Library of Congress Cataloging in Publication Data

Pelikan, Jaroslav Jan, 1923-
    The shape of death.

    "Originally delivered as the Laidlaw lectures,
at Knox College, Toronto, in September, 1959."
    Reprint of the ed. published by Abingdon Press,
New York.
    Bibliography: p.
    Includes index.
    1. Eschatology--History of doctrines--Early
church, ca. 30-600. 2. Death. 3. Immortality--
History of doctrines--Early church, ca. 30-600.
4. Fathers of the church. I. Title.
BT819.5.P44 1978   236   78-6030
ISBN 0-313-20458-6

Reprinted in 1978 by Greenwood Press,
A division of Congressional Information Service, Inc.
88 Post Road West, Westport, Connecticut 06881

Library of Congress catalog card number 78-6030
ISBN 0-313-20458-6

Printed in the United States of America

10 9 8 7 6 5 4 3 2

PREFACE

THE core of the Christian faith is pessimism about life
and optimism about God, and therefore hope for life
in God. Christianity comes into the world with this
message of pessimism and optimism and hope, and
much of the history of early Christian thought consists
in working out the implications of this message for the
Christian understanding of God, man, and the relation
between them. Pessimism about man and optimism
about God—nowhere do they come together more dramatically than in the Christian view of death. As San-
tayana said, "a good way of testing the calibre of a
philosophy is to ask what it thinks of death." The same
test applies to a theology. A theology whose central message is the biography of a crucified Jew cannot avoid
speaking about death, whether it be his death or ours.
This gospel of death gave the early Christians a feeling
for the tragedy of life to meet the pessimism of their
pagan neighbors, and it gave them a buoyancy beyond
the tragedy to meet the optimism of their pagan neighbors. Such sorrow and joy and joy mingled with sorrow
still constitute the appeal of the Christian gospel. Chris-

5

tianity still lays claim to the loyalty of men on the grounds that it can make sense of both life and death because the coming of Jesus Christ in his life and in his death can make them pessimistic about life and optimistic about God and therefore hopeful for life in God.

These five chapters, originally delivered as the Laidlaw Lectures at Knox College, Toronto, in September, 1959, examine some of the forms that this pessimism about life and optimism about God took during the second and third centuries, as the Christian community began to reflect upon the implications of its message. They are based upon the thought of five church fathers from those centuries—Tatian, Clement of Alexandria, Cyprian, Origen, and Irenaeus. The titles of these essays are symbols taken from plane geometry, not because the author is a baptized neo-Pythagorean who sees in the mysteries of line and angle a revelation of the nature of the divine, but because these five figures seem to summarize the several insights into "the shape of death" characteristic of these five Christian theologians. The world in which we live is vastly different from theirs. We look at the stars differently, and at disease, language, history, and many other constitutent parts of life. But we still have to die, just as they did. Hence the Christian description of the shape of death can still make itself heard through a church father from long ago and far away: "and by it he, being dead, yet speaketh."

JAROSLAV PELIKAN

CONTENTS

THE ARC OF EXISTENCE

I

THE ARC OF EXISTENCE

THE Christian answer to man's hope for immortality is both yes and no. Sometimes Christian thought has stressed the yes, less often the no, but both belong to the Christian answer. The *Address to the Greeks* of the second-century church father and heretic Tatian is a harsh and confusing, yet powerful statement of the no in the Christian answer. In answer to man's aspirations and pretensions, Tatian declares that man cannot by his own powers leap across the boundaries of his existence. Whereas certain philosophers promise their ad-

11

herents life after death and describe human existence as a circle without beginning or end, Tatian holds out to his readers the prospect of their own transience. He speaks of "our allotted span passing away." Thus he stresses the no in the Christian gospel of death. Man passes, changes, finishes his span, dies. Not a circle without beginning or end, but an arc, a short segment of the circle with a clearly defined beginning and a definitely prescribed end, would therefore be the proper figure for human life, according to Tatian. Man's life is described by the arc of existence.

The idea of a circle as the shape of life and death is not merely a philosophy of life, but an entire world view. It claims to interpret both man and the cosmos. In describing the arc of existence, Tatian is obliged also to eliminate from view all the circles that classical thought draws to explain the nature of things. He has to portray the gospel as a deliverance not only from sin, but from the supernatural as well; through the gospel life is literally disenchanted. Specifically, Tatian satirizes the zodiac, the "cycle of animals" that has been imposed upon the heavenly spheres as an explanation for the course of human existence. If even animals can qualify for the heavenly dignity of the zodiac, so astrology appears to reason, it would seem certain that man's existence is truly celestial and significant. Refusing to accept the reality of their life and their death, men try to explain the arc of existence as part of a vast celestial circle. Others again try to say that everything this side of the moon is beyond the jurisdiction of divine providence and therefore lies within the purview of man's authority.

These and other efforts to break through the confines of the arc of existence are a refusal to admit that death is final and that man cannot do anything about it. When men try to embellish the arc of existence by extending the ends of the arc either forward or backward, they are rebuffed by the stubborn reality of God and by the unbridgeable difference between God and man. Judged by the theological and philosophical tastes of most Christian theologians, Tatian undoubtedly exaggerates this difference for the sake of a rhetorical point. Surely, as the other fathers being discussed here recognized, there must be some discernible analogy or congruence between the arc of human existence and the lines of the life of God. Yet there are times when men lose sight of the difference between God and man, when they need to be reminded that God is in heaven and man is on earth. At such times it is necessary for a man to remember his origin in the free and arbitrary action of the creating God, as well as his destiny in a death that separates him from the living God. Only in this way can the seriousness of life come to voice.

Justin Martyr, the teacher of Tatian, recognizes that logically it is just as easy to extend the arc of existence backward as forward. The doctrine of the pre-existence of the soul makes as much sense as does the doctrine of the immortality of the soul. In fact, as Justin points out, the two doctrines are closely related; for "if it [the soul] is immortal, it is plainly unbegotten. It is both unbegot-

13

ten and immortal, according to some who are styled Platonists." The logic that links immortality to pre-existence is not prevalent enough to give pre-existence as much circulation among the Greeks and Romans as immortality was beginning to enjoy in the early centuries of our era. As Clement of Alexandria and Origen illustrate, both the classical mind and the Christian mind find it less difficult to grasp the notion of immortality than to ascribe an eternal pre-existence to the human soul. The reasons for this are probably quite complex, but one reason certainly is this: "immortality" really means the supposition that a particular human existence can be extended from seventy to seven hundred to seven thousand years and so on literally ad infinitum, while "pre-existence" seems to deny time altogether. Beneath all such speculations there lies the fundamental human intuition that whatever takes a beginning must also find an end. Therefore the only existence whose arc one can extend into the infinite future is an existence whose arc may likewise be extended into the infinite past—if, that is, phrases like "infinite future" or "infinite past" convey any meaning at all.

With his teacher, Justin, Tatian declares Christian war upon pre-existence as well as upon immortality, in the name of the sovereignty of God. Tatian battles on two fronts simultaneously—on one front against these philosophical notions, on a second front against the ancient Greek legends of how the gods began. "Our God does not have a beginning within time. Only He is without beginning, and He is Himself the beginning of all things." Tatian is arguing here that the elaborate theogonies and divine genealogies of Greek religion past and present are inconsistent with the speculative doctrines of Greek philosophy about the pre-existence of the human soul. The Greeks represent the divine as having a beginning within time, and then they permit the human soul to be without beginning! The fundamental error in the doctrine of the pre-existence of the soul, according to Tatian, is what it says (or fails to say) about God the Creator; therefore it is in error also when it speaks as it does about man the creature. Extending the arc of human existence backward into infinity ascribes to man what only God can possess. Much of Tatian's address is a violent and ofttimes crude manifesto of God's priority over all his creatures. No human soul or spirit or combination of the two can be permitted to arrogate to itself the worship that belongs to the perfect God alone. Ultimately the doctrine of the pre-existence of the human soul is irreconcilable with the doctrine of divine creation. Man cannot stretch the arc of existence all the way to infinity, because infinity belongs only to God and man is to be content with the arc.

In addition to this essentially theological and religious argument against pre-existence, Tatian challenges the doctrine also on another ground, the theory of time that underlies it. Although his argumentation here may not be very profound or original, echoing as it does the common-sense objections of every age to the philosophical interpretation of time, he does manage to use also this argumentation to stress his basic doctrine of change and transience.

Why do you divide time, saying that one part is the past, another the present, and another the future? For how can the future be engaged in passing while the present still exists? As people who are sailing ignorantly suppose that the hills are moving while it is actually the ship that is being carried along, so you do not realize that you are the ones who are passing along, but that time remains as the present as long as its Creator wills that it should exist.

The arc of human existence has a definite point of beginning and an equally definite point of ending, but to give it the illusion of permanence men imagine that time itself is an infinite process of changing in which the human soul does not pass away but stands firm. Thus the illusion of pre-existence rests upon a fundamental confusion, the refusal to accept the reality of change and decay in the life of man.

Man has no right, therefore, to extend the arc of his brief existence backward into the ages or to claim that his soul existed before it entered his body. Yet any such claim is usually a way for man to justify extending the arc in the other direction as well. Man wants to claim pre-existence for his soul because he aspires to immortality; if his soul existed before the brief arc of earthly existence began, it can continue to exist also after that arc has been closed. Or to put the matter as sharply as Tatian does, if the soul does not need an act of the Creator in order to come into existence but pre-existed

16

all along on its own power, then it does not need an act of the Creator to come to life after death but can go on living immortally by its own power. Vigorous though Tatian's polemic against the doctrine of pre-existence may be, his polemic against the doctrine of the natural immortality of the soul is even more explicit.

"Of itself," he writes, "the soul is not immortal, but mortal, O Greeks. Nevertheless, it is capable of not dying. If it does not know the truth, it dies and is dissolved with the body." In antithesis to the claim that the soul is not capable of dying, Tatian maintains that it is both capable of dying and capable of not dying; which of these destinies awaits it depends upon its relation to God. Not within the soul itself, but in the life-giving Spirit of God resides the power to grant life after death. The details of Tatian's doctrine of death are so confusing as to support the suggestion that he is confused about his own teaching. Interpreters have given him credit or blame for an astonishing variety of doctrines. Nevertheless, Tatian does make clear the grounds of his objection to the doctrine of the natural immortality of the soul. To delineate the boundaries of the arc of existence as he draws them, it is necessary to summarize these grounds.

Like his argument against the pre-existence of the soul, Tatian's rejection of natural immortality is fundamentally theocentric. "Not existing before I came to be, I did not know who I was, and existed only in the potentiality of fleshly matter; but having come to be after being nothing, I have through my birth become certain of my existence." This is his case against pre-existence, and in the next sentence he continues: "In the same way, having come to be and through death existing no longer, I shall exist again, just as previously I did not exist but then came to be." As the basis for this expectation he cites his conviction that "God the Sovereign, when He pleases, will restore to its original state the substance that is visible to Him alone." Neither for his original birth out of the nothingness of non-being nor for his ultimate rebirth out of the nothing-ness of death can man take the credit, but it belongs to God's sovereignty and discretion to create a human be-ing in the first place and to re-create him after he has been annihilated by death.

If a man is to find immortality he has to look for it at the source from which his life has originally come, the free and sovereign action of God the Creator. The intent of the Creator was to "make man an image of [His] immortality, so that, as incorruptibility is with God, thus man, participating in God, might have im-mortality also." Whatever immortality a man may ob-tain is thus by participation in the immortality and in-corruptibility of God. In the passage just cited Tatian carries the argument a whole step further by ascribing this creative act to the eternal Word of God, Christ as the heavenly Logos. Both for his pristine immortality, which he lost in the fall, and for his ultimate immor-tality, which he regains in the redemption, man is de-pendent upon the initiative of the divine Logos, who was the principle of creation and who has become, as Jesus Christ, the agent of salvation. Tatian's case against immortality rests upon other grounds as well, some of them specious, others rhetorical, still others quite sound. Yet it seems that the chief reason for his opposition lies in the ease with which a doctrine of natural immortality enables a man to declare his independence from God in Christ. To insist upon the arc of existence and nothing beyond the arc of existence as man's natural lot is to draw a necessary corollary from the confession of the creed that God is the Maker of heaven and earth.

The arc of existence can become more than just an arc if one extends its line to form a circle. Tatian rejects the circle when men use it to talk about pre-existence; he rejects it even more vigorously when men base their hope for immortality upon it. He refuses to listen to the Stoic doctrine that after the conflagration with which the world is to end the same man will rise again and will go on doing the same things he used to do in his former life, be they good or wicked. From this doctrine, half mythological and half philosophical, he tries to disengage the Christian hope for resurrection, life after death, and the restitution of all things. Christians do not hope for an endlessly revolving cycle of useless creation and destruction, but for a single and unrepeatable resurrection, once and for all. A theory of cycles makes it impossible for anything to happen once and for all. The Christian doctrine of history is based upon the conviction that as Christ the Savior came once and for all to accomplish a unique and unrepeatable redemp-

19

tion, so Christ the Judge will come once and for all to execute a final and inevitable judgment. Although the idea of cycles promises immortality beyond the arc of this bounded existence, it actually holds out the prospect of an endless karma from which even the merciful forgetfulness of death is no escape. In antithesis to this, the Christian gospel of death announces to men the gracious message that they will die once and for all.

The Christian gospel of death thus puts a higher estimate upon time and history than does the cycle theory of immortality. It puts a higher estimate also upon the human body. Lurking behind many versions of the doctrine of natural immortality, as Clement of Alexandria declares against the Gnostics, is the supposition that the body is naturally evil and that the soul is to be preferred to it as the part that is naturally good, indeed, as the part that has affinity with the divine. The Christian view of man, especially where it has kept its touch with the realism of the Old Testament, never loses sight of the body in its earnestness about the soul. Tatian's view is even more conscious of the body than are most Christian doctrines of man. According to him, "the human soul is complex, not simple. It is a composite, in order to be manifest through the body. For it [the soul] could never appear by itself, without the body; nor will the flesh rise again without the soul." Soul and body are certainly inseparable in thought; ghosts usually seem to be endowed with bodily, if somewhat shadowy, form. Soul and body are inseparable also in fact and in hope, Tatian asserts. If one of the Greeks maintains that only the soul becomes immortal, "I declare that the flesh also does with it." Still one must ask: What point is there in distinguishing between soul and body at all if they are inseparable? From Tatian's inconsistent use of terms like "soul" and "spirit" it may be concluded that he does not have a clear and definite conception of how the various components of man (however many they may be) fit together.

Meanwhile, he is eager to point out the inconsistencies and absurdities in the teachings of his opponents. He finds the doctrine of natural immortality absurd because it declares that a man who during his lifetime was stupid and feeble acquires new powers after he dies. "It is," he adds, "hard to imagine that the immortal soul, impeded by the members of the body, should acquire more sense when it has emigrated from the body." He seems to mean that death does not add anything to the person, even to his soul, but subtracts something. How then can it be legitimate not only to extend the lines of the arc of existence beyond the point of death, but even to draw them thicker and heavier outside the arc than within it? Similarly, he lampoons the idea that the dead can return, asking sarcastically: "Since during my lifetime I was by no means evil, how is it possible that now when I am dead and impotent, my remains, which are incapable of motion or even of sense, should be able to do something that can be perceived?" Even on the grounds of reason Tatian finds the idea of natural immortality unacceptable. Although he works hard to show the Greeks that the Christian gospel is far superior to the vagaries of their philosophy, he is willing to make use of philosophy when it supports his point; but he does not admit that such a use of philosophy seriously qualifies the strictures he has been voicing. It is, moreover, consistent with his general attitude when Tatian practically ignores those Greek and Roman philosophers who, like himself, emphasize the boundaries of the arc of existence and do not ascribe to man a life beyond the boundaries.

If the arc of existence is the shape of death and its boundaries are the limits of natural human life as it is now constituted by God's creation and man's fall, it seems to follow that there is no intrinsic difference between man and other creatures. Then, at most, man is man and not a cat. Tatian is not afraid to draw this radical conclusion. "The character of man's nature is such that if it is like a temple, God is pleased to dwell in it by the Spirit, His Ambassador. But if it is not such a dwelling, man is superior to the beasts only by virtue of articulate speech; otherwise his way of life is like theirs, as one who is not an image of God." The theory of natural immortality is mistaken when it maintains that by virtue of his rational and immortal soul man is intrinsically better than the beasts; for it is not the rational and immortal soul, but the image of God that sets him apart from the beasts. Unlike some of the early fathers, Tatian does not identify the image of God with the rational, immortal soul. Hence absence from the body does not improve the state of the soul.

The fall of the demons is dramatic proof of this. Completely unencumbered by a body, they led an utterly spiritual life from the moment of their creation. If the nonphysical form of reality were superior to the physical, they would never have fallen. But fall they did, into a death more bitter than the death of the body. Even in their fallen state they have the distinction of not having to die as men do, but this distinction is no advantage, for although they will always be immortal, as they are now, they will not receive the blessings of the life eternal. Thus they "die continually even while they remain alive." Here is a cogent argument against the claim that man's soul must be naturally immortal because it is the superior part of his being. It suggests that there is nothing desirable about living forever. Those who ask for an endless life should realize what they are getting into. Not immortality, but the life eternal, is a good to be pursued and cherished. For Christianity "the life eternal" does not mean living forever in heaven after the arc of existence here on earth has been drawn and completed. It means being alive in God, both now and always. Death as the end of the arc of existence may be dreadful to contemplate, but an infinitely more appalling prospect is the eternal dying of an immortality without God.

The Greeks, of course, are not afraid of death, Tatian comments ironically. They have cultivated the contempt of death as an art, and they claim to be indifferent to its horrors. This claim Tatian meets with a twofold argument. First, he chides the pagans for not fearing death and yet trying to inflict it upon others, specifically upon Christians, as a punishment. Recalling his own experience of near martyrdom at the instigation of the Cynic Crescens, he contrasts the abstract claims of pagan philosophy with the concrete performance of a pagan philosopher. If death is not a threat, why do they threaten Christians with death? Here he states the theme of martyrdom, which recurs throughout early Christian discussions of death. The fathers spoke of death as they did not only because their faith and their experience both taught them that men had to die but because they and their fellow believers had to face the possibility of dying for their faith.

Tatian's second argument is quite out of keeping with the general tenor of his treatise, so much so that one is inclined to read it as a sarcastic apostrophe to Crescens. "If you share our doctrines and say that death is not to be dreaded, do not, like Anaxagoras, die for the sake of an insane pursuit of fame among men, but rather become despisers of death for the sake of the knowledge of God." He is, in effect, pleading with the Greeks not to repudiate their philosophy, but to fulfill it by accepting the doctrines of Christianity. Perhaps it is the recollection of his teacher Justin Martyr that moves him momentarily to look more kindly at the achievements of pagan thought, but it seems more plausible to interpret this passage as a rhetorical outburst. Here Tatian is speaking more profoundly than he may realize; for Christianity does address itself both to the fear of death and to the contempt of death in classical thought, bringing to both its gospel of pessimism about life and optimism about God. Because this is the Christian message, Tatian is right when he says that the Greeks "share our doctrines and say that death is not to be dreaded," even though they do not do so for the sake of the true knowledge of God in Christ.

The message of the church to the Greek world, then, is: Accept the arc of existence and be conformed to the shape of death! Yet there is more to Tatian's gospel than this, more also to his interpretation of death. One who accepts the arc of existence and does not attempt to seize immortality for himself begins to understand the meaning of death more profoundly. Tatian expresses this more profound understanding when, in developing his thesis that the demons go on sinning because they are immortal, he asks: "Is it not so that among the men who follow the demons fewer kinds of sin develop because their life is shortened, while the demons multiply their transgressions because their existence is boundless?" This means that there is nothing good about immortality if that immortality entails separation from God. It means also that under the conditions of human existence death must be regarded as good because it delivers men from a life of steady deterioration and endless sinning. The arc of existence as arc becomes less fearful with the reminder that it is the arc of existence, which is, in Paul Tillich's definition, "rooted both in ethical freedom and in tragic destiny." For death is not only the wages of sin; it is also the end of sin's dominion, the line that God draws to keep the arc of tragic existence from becoming an endlessly revolving circle of tragic

25

existence. This may well be the meaning behind the cryptic primitive utterance of Gen. 3:22: "And now, lest he [man] put forth his hand and take also of the tree of life, and eat, and live for ever." The arc of existence is bad perhaps, but a circle of existence would be a great deal worse.

Thus the core of the Christian faith is pessimism about life and optimisim about God, but this combination produces hope for life in God. Emphasize though he may that existence is an arc, the spokesman for the Christian gospel must describe this arc with hope. In fact, Tatian's very emphasis upon the arc of existence makes it possible for him to speak of the Christian hope, as is evident from the passage quoted earlier:

Not existing before I came to be, I did not know who I was, and existed only in the potentiality of fleshly matter; but having come to be after being nothing, I have through my birth become certain of my existence. In the same way, having come to be and through death existing no longer, I shall exist again, just as previously I did not exist but then came to be. . . . God the Sovereign, when He pleases, will restore to its original state the substance that is visible to Him alone.

Tatian appears to mean that because existence is an arc, bounded at both ends by the vast emptiness of nonbeing, God is able to call a man into actuality out of the potentiality that he alone sees. He did just that when the man was created out of nothing through his birth, and he does it once more when he re-creates the

26

man out of nothing to grant him the life eternal. It is the way of God that he "gives life to the dead and calls into existence the things that do not exist."

Such is the ironic contrast between the two shapes of death, the notion of natural immortality and the Christian description of the arc of existence. The only man to whom God grants the life eternal is the man who refuses to grasp for immortality on his own. God brings men not from life to life with smoothness and ease, but from life to death to life with the pain of childbirth and the pangs of death and the continuing threat of nonexistence hanging over them. Living in hope, therefore, means living by faith in the God who can reach even into the hollowness of nonexistence—indeed, only into the hollowness of nonexistence—to confer life. To live in hope and faith means to recognize the shape of death. "After losing immortality," Tatian says, "men have conquered death by submitting to death in faith." Therefore "everyone who has been conquered may conquer again if he rejects the condition that brings death." The Christian gospel of death affirms the arc of existence and bids men conquer death by submitting to death. It invites them, in the words of Tatian: "Why is it your fate to go on grasping for things and to go on dying over and over again? Die to the world, and repudiate its madness. Live to God, take hold of Him, and lay aside your old nature."

For this invitation to conquer death by submitting to death, Christianity has the highest possible ground and precedent, the life and death of One who "offered

27

up prayers and supplications, with loud cries and tears, to him who was able to save him from death, and he was heard for his godly fear. . . . For the joy that was set before him [he] endured the cross, despising the shame, and is seated at the right hand of the throne of God." It can speak as it does about the arc of existence because its basic message is an existence that formed an arc, from A.D. 1 to A.D. 33. Everything that Christian theology is obliged to say about the Logos before that arc or about the Lord after that arc must be related to Jesus known as the Christ within that arc, or it is not a part of the Christian witness: this is a fundamental axiom for the theological doctrine of the person of Christ. Similarly, everything that Christian theology may say about man before or after the arc of existence must be related to human life as it is lived within the arc of existence, or it is a frivolous evasion of the seriousness of death. The first figure that Christianity draws to describe the shape of death is the arc of existence. This it can continue to learn from the crabbed ascetic Tatian, whose contempt for the world finally proved to be too much even for his fellow monks, so that he was declared a heretic. Heretic though he is, he does teach Christian thought to look with utmost earnestness at the arc of existence.

Yet, as Tatian himself suggests, that is not enough. Characteristically, he draws the lines beyond the arc of existence with such a trembling hand that they are very hard to trace. But draw them he must, and an adequate theology must draw them more carefully than he did. Christianity is, after all, the message of the New Testament as well as of the Old Testament. Tatian does not deliver its message faithfully or adequately when he sets forth what is essentially an Old Testament view of death, with a few overtones from the New Testament. To the human hope for immortality the Christian gospel of death says both no and yes, but it does declare that God's final answer to this hope is a clear and unequivocal yes. Theology has not drawn the shape of death accurately if it has sketched only the arc of existence. The early church is bolder than that. Indeed, it is so bold that, in Clement of Alexandria, it considers the possibility of describing the shape of death as a circle of immortality. The second chapter will sketch the circumference of this circle and try to locate its center.

THE CIRCLE OF IMMORTALITY

II

THE CIRCLE OF IMMORTALITY

CHRISTIANITY has no doctrine of the soul; or, more precisely, it has several. If Christian theology is to make sense of the references to the "soul" in the Bible, it needs a doctrine of the soul from some other source. This need prompts Christian thought to borrow from the speculation of several centuries of Greek thinkers regarding the distinction between body and soul. During the first half of the twentieth century it has become a ritual for Protestant theologians of varying positions to lament this borrowing from Greece,

33

and often with good reason, but the lamentation becomes irresponsible when it gratuitously assumes that instead of borrowing from the Greeks Christian theology should simply have stayed with the "clear teachings of the Bible about the soul." Either Christians are not to speak about the soul in any consistent and reasoned manner at all, or they must be willing to learn about the soul from other places, in addition to their Scriptures.

Immediately the question arises: What limits or judgments does being a Christian theologian impose upon the use of such extra-Christian ideas as the Greek doctrine of the soul? The history of Christian theology has never given a completely satisfying answer to that question, but it has produced several brilliant answers. One brilliant and durable answer is that expounded by Clement of Alexandria. Like Tatian, Clement has been refused admittance to the hall of saints, but for a different reason. Tatian hated creation and culture; Clement loved them too well. From the Greek thought to which he owed so much Clement received the picture of a circle of immortality. His assignment as a Christian intellectual was to Christianize this picture and to make the circle of immortality congruent with the shape of the Christian message. This chapter will examine Clement's ideas in comparison and contrast with the Greek theories behind them, especially those of Middle Platonism, to determine if possible whether Clement taught a circle of immortality and whether he succeeded in making his picture of the shape of death congruent with the Christian gospel of pessimism about life and optimism about God.

Human life must be more than the brief arc of existence. A study of the arc itself shows that it is intended to be more. The very lines of the arc compel one to round them out in a circle. Death acquires an inordinate importance if it is claimed that the total existence of a man is suddenly and irrevocably terminated when he dies. Similarly, the significance of birth is exaggerated if it is claimed that the vast complexity of a human soul and spirit suddenly bursts upon the sky of reality like a nova, without even a glimmer of anticipation. Such intimations as these about the line extending from man's brief hour into the endless hours of God transformed the arc of existence into the circle of immortality. How is the shape of death changed when a thinker comes to believe that the line extending from man's brief hour into the endless hours of God is the line of the cross?

One change is that such a man can no longer speak so glibly as he did before about the pre-existence of the soul. Clement has inherited a doctrine of pre-existence as part of his Platonic tradition, which avers that the soul of man does not begin to exist when his body does. According to the Stoic tradition, on the other hand, body and soul come into existence at the same time. Clement is too much a Christian to take over the Platonic notion uncritically, but he is still too much a Platonist to substitute the Stoic notion for it. He summarizes the opinion of certain philosophers on the origin

35

of the soul: "They do not want to claim that procreation is evil by nature, but that it is so on account of the soul. . . . They maintain that the soul is divine, but is led down from above into the world as into a prison. According to them, the souls that have been embodied must now be purified." This version of pre-existence Clement rejects as inconsistent with the Christian doctrines of divine creation and of divine providence. He writes in a later chapter: "The soul is certainly not sent down from heaven into some worse condition. For God is working everything up to some better condition. But the soul that has chosen the best life, the life that comes from God and righteousness, exchanges earth for heaven."

Clement recognizes that an unqualified theory of the pre-existence of souls cannot be accommodated to Christian teaching. He sees that in certain pagan philosophers, but even more pronouncedly in the Christian heretics who have drawn upon these philosophers, a vision of the circle of pre-existence and immortality leads to blasphemy against God the Creator and against human procreation, the method he has chosen for continuing his creating work. Professing to glorify the pre-existent soul, these heretics finally disparage the body and sex. Clement's second argument against pre-existence reveals even more about the substance of his own thought. The circle of pre-existence and immortality conflicts not alone with creation, but with theodicy. It is the way of God to lead his creatures not from good to worse, but from worse to better. Neither the Christian account of man's origin nor the Christian picture of his destiny can be bent into congruity with the Greek circle of immortality.

Upon deeper reflection, however, Clement finds that both the Christian account of man's origin and the Christian picture of his destiny make some version of the circle of immortality not alone permissible but necessary. The Christian account of man's origin finds the ground of man's being in God's creation, but God accomplishes his creating purpose through mediation; that is why the disparagement of procreation is blasphemy. Yet procreation is only the proximate and temporal means by which God mediates his creation. The agent through whom God accomplishes all his acts of mediation is Christ as the eternal Logos. Although an unqualified theory about the circle of pre-existence is inconsistent with the doctrine of creation, the doctrine of Christ as the eternal Logos necessarily implies that the shape of life and death is more than the simple arc of existence.

We existed before the foundation of the world; because we were destined to be in him, we pre-existed in the sight of God. We are the rational creatures of the Logos of God, on whose account we go all the way back to the beginning; for "in the beginning was the Word." Because the Word was from the beginning, he was and also is the divine ground of all things.

"We existed before the foundation of the world"—but whom does he mean by "we"? He means primarily the

37

elect, those who "were destined to be in him." To them he clearly ascribes a pre-existence that crosses the boundaries of historical, physical existence. Because they are elect in Christ as the eternal Logos, the implication is near at hand that by virtue of rationality other "rational creatures of the Logos of God" may also "go all the way back to the beginning."

If the soul owes its origin to creation through the eternal Logos, the same Logos in whom the saints are predestined, some such implication seems unavoidable. As a Christian philosopher, Clement cannot subscribe to the Platonic doctrine of pre-existence. Such a circle of immortality he refuses to draw. As a Christian philosopher—and the accent here should be on both words, on "Christian" as well as on "philosopher"—Clement feels obliged nevertheless to draw a circle of some kind. Is it enough for Christian theology to erase the circle of immortality from the tablet without drawing a line from the arc of existence back to the ground of all existence in the transcendent Christ? If it is not enough to erase the circle, one must first admire the restraint, and only then lament the concessions, in Clement's version of the doctrine of pre-existence. Clement's doctrine may not be *the* Christian answer, but it is *a* Christian answer.

A corollary of pre-existence in many doctrines of the circle of immortality is the moral superiority of the soul to the body. The arc of existence is a small segment of the circle, and the lowest segment at that, during which the soul is temporarily joined to the body. For all the rest of the circle, the soul is free of physical encumbrance. Having so lofty an origin and destiny, the soul is naturally superior to a body that it occupies for such a brief interval. Besides, the body acts as a temptation and not merely as an encumbrance to the soul. Its appetites and passions continually prompt the soul to forget where it came from and where it is going. For man,

> it seems to me, is like the centaur, a creature from Thessaly, compounded of a rational and [an] irrational part, a soul and a body. The body tills the ground and hastens to it, but the soul presses on to God. Trained in the true philosophy, it hastens to its relatives above, turning away from the desires of the body as well as from labor and fear.

When Clement describes the moral superiority of the soul to the body in such language, the difference between the Christian and the Platonic views of man is hardly discernible. The body has only death to look forward to and meanwhile plods on its way of drudgery. But the soul—ah, the soul! It seems to be here on a brief visit—a holiday or a lost weekend. Its real home is above, where its friends and kinsmen are waiting for its quick return. True philosophy, i.e., Christianity, is aimed at disciplining the soul in preparation for the return. If this were the whole of Clement's teaching, one would have to conclude that the Greek circle of immortality has completely obliterated the shape of the cross. But further examination of Clement's writings

39

uncovers other themes in his speculations about the superiority of the soul to the body. These he gathers together in this summary:

It is conceded that the soul of man is the superior part of man and the body the inferior part. But by nature the soul is not good, nor the body bad. For there are things which are neutral, and among these some are to be preferred and others to be given second rank. Therefore the constitution of man, which belongs to the tangible world, was necessarily composed of things that were diverse but not opposite, namely, of body and soul.

No longer is the body the prison of the soul, nor the soul a homesick angel straining to return. Both body and soul are morally neutral, intrinsically neither good nor evil but susceptible of both good and evil. The Christian doctrine of creation forbids setting body and soul into such an antithesis that they appear alien to each other. The relation between them is a matter of "both-and," not of "either-or." They are indeed diverse, but diverse within one genus, and though recognition of the diversity between them requires the assignment of a greater value to the soul than to the body, such a value judgment dare not transform "both-and" into "either-or." Current psychological and theological fashion would be inclined to emphasize the "both-and" even more than Clement did, to the point perhaps of not preferring the soul to the body at all or even of refusing to make so sharp a distinction between them in the first place. Nevertheless, the answer formulated by Clement provides a good opportunity to watch the Christian and the classical doctrines of man in combination and collision. His answer seems to be that whatever differences of color there may be between the arc of existence and the circle of immortality, the arc belongs to the circle and must not be described in a dotted line.

If, despite death, the arc of existence belongs to the circle of immortality and must not be described in a dotted line, physical existence too must have a value proper to it. Although it does not have the same value that the soul has, the body too is a worthy thing. Clement is called upon to defend this thesis against Christian heretics who, in the name of Christianity and Platonism, denigrate the body and sex. Clement defends Christianity against Platonism on other issues, but here he has the opportunity to defend both Christianity and Platonism against their heretical distorters.

Since these so-called Christians cast aspersions upon the body, let them learn that the harmonious functioning of the body also has something to contribute to that understanding which produces a well-rounded person. Therefore, in the third book of *The Republic* Plato, whom they cite so loudly as support for their disparagement of procreation, says: "For the harmony of the soul it is necessary to take care of the body." By this he who proclaims the message of truth is able to live, and to live well.

Clement's recognition of an agreement between Platonism and Christianity on this question is sound, at least to a point. Cultivation of the body does belong

41

to the world view, if not always to the religion or the philosophy, of the civilized Greek. As Clement's quotation from Plato proves, an emphasis upon the care and training of the body is not necessarily inconsistent with the view that the life of the rational soul is more exalted than merely physical existence. It has been claimed that Plato reproduces this emphasis from the gymnastic tradition in Greek art and music, but that his genuine position comes closer to that of the heretics whom Clement is denouncing. Nevertheless, Werner Jaeger seems to have summarized Plato's view perfectly: "God gave us gymnastics and music together, the inseparable unity of paideia. They are not separable as physical training and intellectual education. They are forces which mould the spirited and the rational sides of human nature."

Also in his treatment of this question, however, Clement does manage to go beyond Platonism. Believing that Christianity is the correction and the fulfillment, not the negation, of the classical spirit, Clement can argue simultaneously on the grounds of Greek intellectualism and on the grounds of the Christian gospel.

Those who run down created existence and vilify the body are wrong. They do not consider that the frame of man was formed erect for the contemplation of heaven, that the organization of the senses tends to knowledge, and that the members and parts are arranged for good not for pleasure. Therefore this dwelling place becomes capable of containing the soul, which God holds in the highest regard;

and it is honored by [the presence of] the Holy Spirit through the sanctification of both soul and body, perfected with the perfection of the Savior.

Classical writers frequently argue for the superiority of man on the basis of his erect posture; biblical writers urge their readers to greater loyalty on the basis of the indwelling of the Holy Spirit and the incarnation of the Son of God in a human body. To appreciate how Clement draws the circle of immortality, one must observe that in Clement's thought these two types of argumentation coincide. Both support the Christian-Platonic regard for the body as well as for the soul, in opposition to a heretical contempt for the body as the prison of the soul.

The arc of existence may be the lower edge of the circle of immortality, but it still belongs to the circle. Accepting the circle of immortality as the shape of death dare not mean a contempt for this body and its life. It must mean the responsible use of the body as a gift from God the Creator, as a possession shared with Christ the Savior, as the dwelling place of the Holy Spirit. Clement shows a similar sense of responsibility when he speaks about the attitude of the Christian pilgrim toward the world. If the Gnostic exaltation of the soul over the body is combined with the Christian contempt for the transient world, the combination emerges as a denial of the world that borders on a denial of creation itself. The heresy of Marcion and of Christian Gnostics generally is perhaps the best illustration of how deeply this combination can cut into the central affirmations of the Christian faith. Just as the circle of immortality does not give the soul a warrant to vilify the body that God has created, so the circle must not become a pretext for indifference to the world into which God the Creator has placed the soul.

Now the soul of the wise man and Gnostic [that is, the Christian intellectual], as sojourning in the body, conducts itself towards the body not with inordinate affections, but gravely and respectfully as about to leave the tabernacle if the time of departure should summon. "I am a stranger in the earth, and a sojourner with you," it is said. And hence Basilides says that he apprehends that the elect are strangers to the world, being supramundane by nature. But this is not the case! For all things are of one God. And no one is a stranger to the world by nature, their essence being one, and God one. But the elect man dwells as a sojourner, knowing all things to be possessed and disposed of; and he makes use of the things which the Peripatetics make out to be the threefold good things. The body, too, as one sent on a distant pilgrimage, uses inns and dwellings by the way. It has care of the things of the world, of the places where it stops; but it leaves its dwelling place and property without excessive emotion. Readily it follows Him who leads it away from life. By no means and on no occasion does it turn back, but gives thanks for its sojourn and blesses [God] for its departure, embracing the mansion that is in heaven.

In support of this remarkable summary of the Christian attitude toward the world Clement cites the apostle

Paul, the Sicilian dramatist Epicharmus, and the Greek lyric poet Pindar. These diverse authorities all agree that though heaven is better, earth can be very good indeed, and that though the soul is superior, the body is not to be despised. "For all things are of one God. And no one is a stranger to the world by nature, their essence being one, and God one."

Yet though the world is good, it is also good to die. As Epicharmus says:

Endowed with pious mind, you will not, in dying,
Suffer aught evil. The spirit will dwell in heaven above.

Death, too, has its place in God's grand design, in the circle of immortality. Not because he disdains the world, which is still God's creature, but because he is in training for the hour of his death, the Christian philosopher refuses to involve himself unduly in the entanglements of the present life. The circle of immortality is a complete circle, and the present life on earth truly belongs to the circle. Yet there is more to the circle than the present life on earth, vastly more. Recognizing the circle of immortality as the shape of death means living at the perimeter of the circle and knowing that death is the way to its upper reaches. Clement follows classical precedent in defining death as "the separation of the soul from the body." He can go even further and speak of death as "the dissolution of the chains that bind the soul to the body." Clearly death is a liberation from the bonds of the present life; it is not an evil, but a good.

What of man's natural horror before the reality of his impending death? If death is an unadulterated good, what does the apostle Paul mean when he speaks of death as "the last enemy" and as "wages of sin"? Do not such terms express man's natural horror of death and make it clear that the fear of death may not be waved aside by a simple reference to the circle of immortality as the shape of death? Clement seems to have made the Christian philosopher so detached and calm in the face of death that he no longer appears human. Clement interprets the biblical language about the evil of death as a reference to sin or "spiritual death" rather than to death as "the separation of the soul from the body." For this he has substantial warrant in biblical usage, as he demonstrates in his citation of Romans 6. He argues that death is not an evil if one considers it in relation to the nature and destiny of the body and the soul. Such consideration reverses the usual definitions of "life" and of "death," so that

death is the fellowship of the soul in a state of sin with the body, and life the separation from sin. . . . The severance, therefore, of the soul from the body, made a lifelong study, produces in the philosopher such a gnostic alacrity that he is easily able to bear natural death, which is the dissolution of the chains that bind the soul to the body.

In a statement like this the difference between Christian faith and classical philosophy is overshadowed by the harmony between them. Christianity seems to add two elements to the philosophical contempt of death. First, the Christian doctrine of sin makes death even more desirable because dying brings release not only from pain and striving, but also from sin and temptation. Second, Christian eschatology further softens the terror of death by holding forth the prospect of a better life beyond the grave. All of this is true and Christian, but Clement's circle of immortality seems to miss something about the shape of death that is present in Tatian's description of the arc of existence. Is it not also true and Christian that death is an evil, embittering life and ruining hope? Although believers are told not to mourn as do those who have no hope, is there perhaps a mourning that is proper for those who do have hope? The absence of this existential pathos from Clement's drawings of the shape of death gives them an unrealistic, and therefore an unchristian, distortion of perspective. Tatian's drawing of the arc of existence prompts one to remark that the Old Testament does not say everything there is to say about the shape of death. In sketching the circle of immortality according to Clement, it is necessary to say that the Christian picture of the shape of death dare never ignore the Old Testament; for if it does, the theocentric realism that this section of the Christian Scriptures has always contributed to the doctrine of man will be absent, and philosophical idealism will easily slide into its place.

When the perspective of the Old Testament yields

to the influence of philosophical idealism, theology has great difficulty handling the question of time and history. There are no full-scale studies of Clement's understanding of time, and few studies of the Christian views of time generally. In much of his writing Clement gives the indication that he has been influenced by Greek more than by Hebrew thought in his historical thinking. Thus he can speak of Atlas as symbolizing "the fixed sphere, or better perhaps, motionless eternity." When eternity is interpreted this way, it is difficult to think of time in any other metaphor than the cycle. Although some theologians have obviously gone too far in their generalizations on this point, classical historical thought did operate with this as one of its basic metaphors for time and history. As Cochrane has summarized the contrast:

Antiquity thought of [the forces of history] as, on the whole circuitous; representing them accordingly either as an "upward and downward path" or as a "wheel." . . . For classical idealism [the theory of cycles] takes shape as a belief in the endless reiteration of "typical" situations, a belief which does the grossest injustice to the unique character and significance of the individual historical event. . . . [Augustine] bears witness to the faith of Christians that, notwithstanding all appearances, human history does not consist of a series of repetitive patterns, but marks a sure, if unsteady, advance to an ultimate goal. As such, it has a beginning, a middle, and an end.

Thus Christian thought rejects the cyclical view of

history because this view does not allow for the single and unrepeatable event of Jesus Christ. From the Old Testament Christian thought has learned to look upon time and history as the stage for God's activity. As the cyclical theory of history is finally incompatible with the Christian view of the person of Christ, so the circle of immortality is incompatible with the Christian view of the work of Christ. Nor can the shape of the cross and the circle of immortality be made congruent by the declaration that Christ has made immortality possible, unless this declaration is accompanied by a radical redefinition of the very meaning and content of "immortality." "Born of the Virgin Mary . . . was crucified, dead, and buried"—here the church confesses its faith by reciting the crucial points in the life story of its Lord. To him, if to anyone, Christians would have a right to apply the circle of immortality. Before his birth from the Virgin Mary he dwelt with his Father from eternity, and after his death under Pontius Pilate he rose from the dead and ascended to his Father, with whom he lives for eternity. A grand and cosmic circle is his life, in which the years A.D. 1 to A.D. 33 are a mere episode.

Some early Christian language about Christ does flirt with the possibility of describing the shape of his life and being as a grand and cosmic circle. Loss of contact with biblical seriousness about time and history does threaten to distort the perspective of Christian pictures of Christ. It does this in the early centuries of theological history, and it continues to do this whenever the crucial points of birth and death in his life become

49

mere dots on the circumference of a large circle. Repeatedly, Christian thought about Jesus as the Christ has had to repossess its seriousness about time and history. In the thought of Athanasius, for example, both the gravity of the danger and the resources for meeting the danger are evident. The very same danger affects Christian thought about the shape of death. Beguiled by the grand circle of Christ's eternal life, Christian theology can speak of his birth and death with a casualness that is almost blasphemous. Under the same spell, it can likewise speak of the death of the believer so nonchalantly or so heroically that those who have known the *Angst* of their mortality feel guilty or deprived because they cannot face the prospect of their own dissolution all that stoically. Then theology and preaching need to be reminded of the bloody sweat in Gethsemane and of the "Eli, Eli." The gospel does not show a way around the fear of death, but a way through the fear of death to life in God.

On several counts, then, Clement's drawing of the shape of death calls for further thought. Time is not a circle, and neither is eternity. The life of man in time and eternity does not describe a circle. Some other figure for the shape of death must be found that will give expression to the valid insights in the circle of immortality. The fourth chapter of this book will describe how the most creative mind of the early church, Origen, attempts to break through the top of the circle so that God may take a more direct role than the circle of immortality permits. Origen bends the circle of immortality into the parabola of eternity, both of whose arms reach into the endless years of God. The parabola as a picture of the shape of death is a way of preserving the valid insights in Clement's theory and yet of including more of the biblical perspective. This contrast between the two shapes of death is in keeping with the fundamental difference between the speculative thought of Clement and the much more exegetical and traditional thought of Origen. Clement does indeed profess to derive his teachings from Scripture and tradition; but, as Hanson says, "When we examine the contents of this tradition [which Clement claims to be citing], we find it to consist of theological speculations which have a suspiciously Alexandrian ring about them, and which we cannot possibly imagine to have emanated from our Lord and his apostles."

None of this alters or diminishes the greatness of Clement's contribution to early Christian thought about the shape of death. The Bible has no original and consistent doctrine of the soul. Yet the Bible does speak about the soul, and thus it obliges its interpreters to speak about the soul too. Clement's depiction of the circle of immortality is one attempt to make sense of what the Bible says about the soul, and to do so with the aid of Greek categories and ideas, particularly those from Middle Platonic and Stoic philosophy. The Greek tradition does agree with the Christian in describing the life of man in the world between birth and death as a pilgrimage, whose ultimate goal is the heavenly City of God. It is therefore fitting that Clement closes

51

his description of the death of the body and the life of the soul with these words:

I shall pray the Spirit of Christ to wing me to my Jerusalem. The Stoics say that heaven is properly a city, but that places here on earth are not cities; they may be called so, but they are not. For a city is an important thing, and the people a decorous body, a multitude of men regulated by law as the church is regulated by the Word [of God]—a city on earth impregnable, free from tyranny, a product of the divine will on earth as in heaven. Images of this city the poets create with their pen. . . . And we know Plato's city placed as a pattern in heaven.

THE TRIANGLE OF MORTALITY

III

THE TRIANGLE OF MORTALITY

CHRIST comes into the world to teach men how to die. The purpose of his coming is indeed "that they might have life, and have it abundantly." But the only life he offers is life through his cross. He calls upon men to accept their mortality and, by accepting it, to live through him. The gospel of Jesus Christ is thus the gospel about human mortality, in contrast with human gospels about immortality. A symbol of how central the idea of mortality is in the Christian gospel is the Latin word *mortalitas* itself. There are

55

very few instances of *mortalitas* in classical Latin; Cicero, for example, uses the word once or twice. In ecclesiastical Latin, however, the word becomes more frequent. Cyprian even puts the word into the title of one of his shorter treatises, *De mortalitate,* written probably in A.D. 252 to comfort Christians amid the ravages of a terrible pestilence; the word *mortalitas,* as he uses it, means not alone "mortality," but the pestilence itself. In this treatise, *On the Mortality,* Cyprian summarizes much of early Christian thought about mortality and the life eternal.

Both the arc of existence and the circle of immortality describe the shape of death with bold strokes, but neither of these figures manages to bring together the horizontal and the vertical dimensions of death into any but an accidental juxtaposition. The arc of existence does relate human living and dying to God, but it cannot draw the horizontal line of life after death. On the other hand, the circle of immortality successfully draws the line that extends from temporal to eternal existence, but it draws that line so well that the vertical dimension of dying to God and receiving life from him again seems to disappear from perspective. Cyprian seeks to do justice to both the horizontal and the vertical dimension of death. Therefore the most appropriate geometrical image to describe his picture of the shape of death appears to be the triangle. The base of the triangle represents his efforts to include the horizontal dimension, the apex of the triangle symbolizes his stress upon the vertical dimension. Thus Cyprian goes beyond both

Tatian and Clement of Alexandria when he includes both the horizontal and the vertical in describing the shape of death as a triangle of mortality.

The base of the triangle stands for the horizontal dimension of death, those aspects of mortality which accentuate the continuity between man and man or between this life and the next, all those points to which it is possible to draw a straight horizontal line from the point of death. Cyprian locates several such points in drawing the triangle of mortality. It is significant that for this horizontal line there are many parallels in the classical "consolation literature" that comes from Greece to Rome through Cicero and becomes a recognized genre of Latin literature well before Cyprian. Each of the solaces that Cyprian expresses to his fellow believers in this horizontal dimension occurs in non-Christian writers before Cyprian, for they summarize the wisdom and comfort that men have gathered about the meaning of death. He gives to these "solaces" his own special Christian interpretation; what is more, the horizontal dimension is not all there is to the triangle of mortality. In spite of these important differences, Cyprian shows that Christians too may avail themselves of the consolations to be found in the natural order at the base of the triangle.

Whenever death comes, one consolation is always the vast and brilliant company of those who have suffered the same fate. The proverbs and the wise men of many nations say that misery loves company. Especially is this true in the hour of bereavement. Even the New Testa-

ment comforts believers with the assurance: "No temptation has overtaken you that is not common to man." It
is easy to forget that mortality is the common lot of all
men, and there is some consolation in realizing this.
There is also some disappointment. Like falling in love,
dying is an intensely personal experience. Rationally,
one knows that it has happened many times before to
many others, but one cannot believe that it has ever
been quite like this before. Cyprian's readers find embarrassment in the wholesale ravages of mortality for
another reason as well.

It troubles some [Christians] that we have this mortality
in common with others [i.e., pagans]. But what in this world
do we not have in common with others as long as this flesh,
in accordance with the law of our original birth, still remains common to us? As long as we are here in the world,
we are united with the human race in equality of the flesh.
. . . Thus when the earth is barren with scanty production
famine excepts no one; thus when a city has been taken by
a hostile attack, bondage ruins all its inhabitants together
. . . ; and we share with others every ailment of our members
as long as this common flesh is borne in the world.

Reminding his readers of the universality of death,
Cyprian also counsels them not to forget their responsibilities. The plague was apparently providing many
with an excuse for moral negligence, but Cyprian interprets it as a searching judgment

whether the well care for the sick, whether relatives dutifully love their kinsmen as they should, whether masters show compassion to their ailing slaves, whether physicians do not desert the afflicted begging their help, whether the violent repress their violence, whether the greedy, even through the fear of death, quench the ever insatiable fire of their raging avarice, whether the proud bend their necks, whether the shameless soften their effrontery, whether the rich, even when their dear ones are perishing and they are about to die without heirs, bestow and give something!

The realization of a common mortality ought to bring with it the realization of a mutual responsibility. Cyprian sees impending death as a crisis that brings out in a man what he really is, and he urges his readers not to surrender to the license and the selfishness that so easily beset men in such a crisis. This is not a uniquely Christian sentiment. It belongs to the horizontal dimension of death and comes from the recognition that even in his mortality man is a social being, with duties and responsibilities from which he may not be excused even by impending death. Surely this recognition belongs in a Christian picture of the shape of death, and the point Cyprian makes is a valid one for all men in their common mortality. That is why it is so widely distributed in the literature of death and consolation.

Even more widely distributed in that literature is the notion that death is a rest from the labor and the sorrow of life. A stock argument in the Greek and Latin consolations is to catalogue the ills to which man is subject and to describe death as the restful cessation of them all. When Cyprian takes over this argument, his Christian theology makes it impossible for him to apply the argument as generally as the consolations do. "This mortality," he writes, "is a bane to the Jews and pagans and enemies of Christ: to the servants of God it is a salutary departure. . . . The just are called to refreshment, the unjust are carried off to torture." Use of the term "rest" for death is by no means restricted to Christians, as both Latin literature and Latin inscriptions show. Despite biblical precedent and great popularity among later Christians, the idea has nothing peculiarly Christian about it; for it is essentially a part of the horizontal dimension of death, and it may provide consolation for the dying or the mourning without reference to any god, Christian or pagan. If death is a rest for the believer, it seems to be a rest for everyone, believer or not. Yet Cyprian repudiates such universalism, and therefore he promises the rest and refreshment of death to believers while he threatens others with the endless torture of damnation.

There is nothing uniquely Christian about statements like these either: "We pass by death to immortality, nor can eternal life succeed unless it has befallen us to depart from here. This is not an end, but a passage and, the journey of time being traversed, a crossing over to eternity." Again, combining this with the notion of rest, Cyprian says: "Then do the servants of God have peace, then do they have a free, then a tranquil repose, when we on being released from the storm of the world have sought the harbor of our abode and eternal security, when on this death being accomplished we have come to immortality." Parallels have been assembled from both Cicero and Seneca to show that Stoic thought has recourse to many of these same arguments and metaphors. Nor does all this become Christian by the mere ritual of inserting the names of God and Christ at appropriate intervals. Even with those names the notion of death as a crossing over into eternity and immortality is part of the horizontal dimension of death. The soul of man is so constituted that when the man dies, it slides across the boundary between time and eternity and goes right on living. To be or become immortal, such a soul has no need of any divine intervention; its immortality is standard equipment. It is perhaps symptomatic of how completely the circle of immortality has replaced the triangle of mortality in the Christian picture of the shape of death that the notion of the translation of the soul from time into eternity would probably be recognized by many as the most characteristically Christian metaphor for death. Cyprian does not set it forth as such, but he does use it alongside other metaphors that belong to the base of the triangle and the horizontal dimension of death.

A closely related metaphor is the picture of death as the soul's return to its native land. The picture appears in Cyprian's peroration. "What man, after having been abroad, would not hasten to return to his native land? Who, when hurrying to sail to his family, would not more eagerly long for a favorable wind that he might more quickly embrace his dear ones? . . . Why do we not hasten and run, so that we can see our country, so that we can greet our parents?" Now this carries an echo of the unforgettable words of the Epistle to Diognetus: "They [Christians] dwell in their own countries, but simply as sojourners. As citizens, they share in all things with others, and yet endure all things as if foreigners. Every foreign land is to them as their native country, and every land of their birth as a land of strangers." Any Christianity that is completely at home in the world has forgotten the alienation between the world as it is and the world as God intended it. Therefore death is indeed the return of the native to the land of his birth. To die does mean to shake off the dust of this foreign land and to cross over into one's true home. Anyone who contemplates his present exile and his eternal home is understandably filled with a longing for his native land and an alacrity to go there as soon as possible.

Taken by itself, however, even this vision of the eternal fatherland scans only the horizontal dimension of death. The New Testament employs this vision, too, but it takes pains to describe both the horizontal and the vertical dimension when it says of Abraham: "He sojourned in the land of promise, as in a foreign land. . . . For he looked forward to the city which has foundations, whose builder and maker is God." As Clement of Alexandria recognized, the only "otherworldliness" that is consistent with the Christian faith is the intuition that man is not essentially a stranger in this world, since both man and the world are creatures of God. Man is a stranger in this world as it now is existentially, because both man and the world are alienated from their Creator. It is never enough, therefore, to describe death as a return to the native land, unless such a description also measures the vertical dimension of death. There is a horizontal dimension; the triangle does have a base, but that base subtends an angle, the apex of the triangle. To comprehend the triangle of mortality as the shape of death means to take both its dimensions, for without the vertical dimension none of the points on the base can explain even the horizontal dimension. As he sought to express the patience and comfort of the Scriptures to his readers, Cyprian looked at the apex of the triangle too.

Describing the vertical dimension of the triangle, Cyprian reminds his readers near the beginning of his treatise:

The Lord predicted that these things would come through the exhortation of His provident voice, instructing and teaching and preparing and strengthening the people of His church to all endurance of things to come. . . . Behold the things which were spoken of are coming to pass, and since the things which were foretold are coming to pass, there will follow also whatsoever were promised.

A little later he asks: "God promises immortality and eternity to you [upon] leaving this world, and do you doubt?" It is not enough to realize that death is the common lot of all mankind, or that the wise men of the past have described universal mortality. The believer lives not by the accumulated wisdom of the centuries, but by the revelation of the will and the promises of

63

God. When he reflects upon his mortality, therefore, he may find a certain limited solace in the bond this gives him with all men everywhere; but the true ground of his consolation is in God. When the time of troubles comes, he sees it as the fulfillment of divine predictions, and hence he is not surprised or shocked at its severity. These predictions are actually part of a divine promise; hence the fulfillment of the prediction harbingers the realization of the promise.

Thus the apex of the triangle is essential to the shape of death. For as the believer goes into the time of troubles he finds the fulfillment of God's predictions; and from this same God he then receives the fulfillment of his promises. He dies to God, and then lives again from God. Cyprian's language, just quoted, makes clear that he is not speaking primarily about an external and literal correspondence between biblical predictions and historical events, nor about an intellectual assurance based upon the possession of saving information concerning God's future plans. He places more stress upon promises than upon predictions; he wants to arouse trust and not merely to convey data. Therefore he argues: "How absurd it is and how perverse that, while we ask that the will of God be done, when God calls us and summons us from this world, we do not at once obey the command of His will!" Mortality belongs to the ways that the God of promise uses to carry out his plans for men. Faith in him means trust that death, too, has its place in his design. The daily prayer that his will may be done on earth as it is in heaven is based upon that trust. Because trust in God even at the hour of death is more than the expectation of immortality, the Christian picture of the shape of death must have a vertical dimension, even when it uses figures and ideas like immortality or deliverance.

Deliverance, too, looks different when it is seen in the vertical dimension. The return of the wayfarer to his long home may make good sense without any clear notion of man's relation to God; so may the translation of the soul into immortality. In Cyprian's hands these notions take on additional meaning, for it is God who does the delivering and the translating. In language that resembles and yet does not resemble the classical consolations, Cyprian calls the roll of the temptations and dangers to which believers are subject in this life, and he chides his readers for ignoring what God is doing through the present crisis.

We are improvident, beloved brethren, and ungrateful for divine favors, and we do not recognize what is being granted us. Behold, the virgins are departing in peace, going safely with their glory, not fearing the threats of the antichrist and his corruptions and his brothels. Boys are escaping the danger of their unsettled age; they are coming happily to the reward of their continency and innocence. No longer does the delicate matron dread the racks, having by a speedy death gained escape from the hands and tortures of the hangman.

What saves this from being a moralistic and rather ascetic harangue is Cyprian's clear-eyed recognition that

65

it is God that grants the deliverance from these moral perils, indeed, that God is himself the deliverance. One may call the loss of a maiden's honor "a fate worse than death" in the Victorian phrase only if one is sure that God is the one who by death delivers her from such a fate.

To this stock Christian solace Cyprian adds a special emphasis, present also in Tatian and in Irenaeus.

We find that Enoch also, who pleased God, was transported, as Divine Scripture testifies in Genesis and says: "And Enoch pleased God and was not seen later because God took him." This was to have been pleasing in the sight of God: to have merited being transported from this contagion of the world. But the Holy Spirit teaches also through Solomon that those who please God are taken from here earlier and more quickly set free, lest, while they are tarrying too long in this world, they be defiled by contacts with the world.

There appears to be no explicit warrant for this last idea in those books of the Bible which Protestants accept as canonical; but there is explicit warrant for it in the Wisdom of Solomon, which seems to be speaking of Enoch: "Being perfected in a short time, he fulfilled long years; for his soul was pleasing to the Lord, therefore he took him quickly from the midst of wickedness." Cyprian bases his exhortation upon this very text, which he quotes elsewhere in his writings too as proof that through death, even through an early death, God rescues men from a life of endless sinning. Canonical or not, this idea has unmistakable authenticity and belongs to any mature Christian interpretation of death as deliverance.

Cyprian can speak of this deliverance with such a vigorous accent because he still shares the attitude of the primitive church toward the world.

If the walls of your house were tottering from decay, if the roof above were shaking, if the house now worn out, now weary, were threatening imminent ruin with its framework collapsing through age, would you not leave with all speed? . . . Behold, the world is tottering and collapsing and is bearing witness to its ruin, not now through age, but through the end of things; and you are not thanking God, you are not congratulating yourself that, rescued by an earlier departure, you are being freed from ruin and shipwrecks and threatening disasters!

Ever since the first Christian died, as the language of I Thessalonians 4 shows, the end of history and the end of an individual life stand in a significant but confusing relationship for Christian thought. As the expectation that history is about to end recedes in prominence, individual death takes over many of the functions previously assigned to this expectation in Christian hope and faith. The thought of both Cyprian and his master Tertullian illustrates this. Often they think of deliverance as the rapture of the church at the end of history, but sometimes as the death of the believer and his rescue from a world that seems likely to outlive him. Whichever of these it is, deliverance is an act of God's intervention, not the pinnacle of man's achievement.

67

The same is true of another metaphor in Cyprian's book *On the Mortality,* the metaphor of death as victory. "Unless a battle has gone before," he argues, "there cannot be a victory; when a victory has been won in the conflict of battle, then a crown also is given to the victors." In the light of Cyprian's theology, it does not seem to be straining his language to emphasize that the crown is given (*datur*) to the victors and that therefore it is God who does the giving. Such an emphasis is consistent also with the usage of the New Testament, in which almost every instance of this metaphor "crown of victory" carries the connotation that God crowns the victors. Deeper reflection would lead to the proposition that God not only crowns the victors but is himself the victor, so that any victory men may win is in fact a participation in the divine victory that has already been accomplished in Christ. Even without this additional note, however, the motif of victory belongs to the vertical dimension in Cyprian's triangle of mortality. That is clearly the implication of a statement like this: "For the battle a fresh and numerous army of great strength is being gathered, which, entering service in the time of the mortality [pestilence], will fight without fear of death when the battle comes."

A closely related motif is the metaphor of death as a "summons." "Let us show," Cyprian admonishes his readers, "that this is what we believe, so that we may not mourn the death even of our dear ones and, when the day of our own summons comes, without hesitation but with gladness we may come to the Lord at His call." The classic instance of such a response to the divine summons is Simeon, who was "happy at the death that was now at hand and untroubled at the approaching summons." It seems that Cyprian was the first man in the history of the Latin language to use the word *arcessitio,* "summons," for death. Since then it has become a euphemism to speak of death as a "summons," even as a "summons to higher service," among devout people. Cyprian is not so genteel, however, and his use of this metaphor is intended to emphasize the call and initiative of the sovereign God. Euphemisms for death like "passing on" or "crossing over" usually carry connotations of the horizontal dimension in the shape of death. To Cyprian the idea of the summons connotes the authority of the Supreme Judge to order a man into his presence and to demand an account from him of all that he has been and done. Far from mitigating the severity of death, as much symbolic language about dying does, this metaphor aggravates it by calling attention to the vertical dimension in the shape of death, the irresistible call of the Summoner.

Of all the ways Cyprian uses to emphasize the vertical dimension in the shape of death, however, none can compare in importance with the idea of "going to Christ." Near the beginning of his treatise he remonstrates with those Christians who fear death: "It is for him to fear death who is unwilling to go to Christ. It is for him to be unwilling to go to Christ who does not believe that he is beginning to reign with Christ." At the very end of the treatise he urges his readers to con-

69

sider the saints in the church triumphant: "To these, beloved brethren, let us hasten with eager longing. Let us pray that it may befall us speedily to be with them, speedily to come to Christ." Between these two passages Cyprian sounds this theme several times, indicating thereby that in the language of the early church dying with Christ and being raised with Christ form a decisive part of the Christian picture of the shape of death. "Why do you," he chides his readers, "who are destined to be with Christ and secure in the promise of the Lord, not rejoice that you are called to Christ?" "We should," he says elsewhere, "earnestly desire and wish to hasten to Christ aided by a death coming more speedily." Nor is this repeated phrase "to Christ" a mere bit of pious rhetoric, for Cyprian knows that the Christ of whom he speaks is "our Lord and our God."

Yet what does it mean specifically to "go to Christ?" What makes this way of speaking about death more meaningful than "going to rest" or, above all, "going to God" would be? Cyprian becomes more specific about this question at several places in the treatise. To die, he says, means "to be changed and reformed to the image of Christ and to the dignity of heavenly grace." The context of these words indicates that in this passage he means the heavenly image of Christ, to which the faithful are to be changed and reformed at their death; he does not mean the image of Christ's cross and death, to which, according to the New Testament, the faithful are to be conformed already in this life. This latter motif appears in a passage like this: "We are firmly expressing

70

our faith and, having endured suffering, are advancing to Christ by the narrow way of Christ. . . . Let him be afraid to die who is not listed under the cross and passion of Christ." Such statements make it clear that the Christ to whom believers go in death is the Christ who has first gone to death for them. The ground of their confidence in Christ is his saving deed on the cross. His death makes their death bearable.

How? Cyprian does not usually specify how Christ's death changes human death; he merely says that it does. The closest he comes to specifying the precise connection between Christ's death and man's is the following commentary on I Thessalonians 4:

He [the apostle] says that those are sorrowful at the death of their dear ones who have no hope. But we who live in hope and believe in God and have faith that Christ suffered for us and rose again, abiding in Christ and rising again through him and in him, why are we ourselves either unwilling to depart hence from this world, or why do we mourn and grieve for our departing ones as if they were lost?

Believers are those who have become partakers of Christ's passion and death. They believe that Christ suffered "for us," which may mean either "in our stead" or merely "for our benefit." Through faith in his suffering "for us" they "abide" in Christ; thus they rise again through him and in him. Therefore they may confidently "come in joyful security to Christ, with whom we are to conquer and reign for eternity." All the great themes of atonement through the passion,

71

death, and resurrection of Christ are present here, but they remain undeveloped.

So undeveloped do these themes remain that after this trenchant summary of the incorporation of the believer into the suffering, dying, and rising Christ, Cyprian continues: "If we believe in Christ, let us have faith in his words and promises." The words and promises of Christ do indeed form an essential part of the faith and consolation of believers as they live in the triangle of mortality. But even the most precious of these words and promises derive their comforting power from the saving deeds of Christ, his suffering, dying, and rising. Cyprian himself says that this is so, but he does not yet have the conceptual apparatus to formulate this as clearly or as convincingly as he formulates the need for the power of Christ against the power of death. In clear straight lines he draws the triangle of mortality as the shape of death. Both the horizontal and the vertical dimensions of the triangle are evident. The base of the triangle is man's justified hope for a continuing life after the death of his body, and the apex of the triangle is the believer's hope for divine intervention to grant him the life after death that he cannot achieve for himself. So far, so good—but not quite good enough, or at least not quite profound enough.

To draw the shape of death, Christian theology must go beyond the triangle of mortality, as it must go beyond the arc of existence and the circle of immortality. The triangle simply imposes the apex, with its lines of extension, upon the base. It therefore exaggerates the angularity of the connection between the two. Christian thought needs a figure for the shape of death that will emphasize the continuity between man's life and God's life as clearly as the circle of immortality does, yet will represent the crisis of life and death as dramatically as the arc of existence does. The figure must symbolize both the continuity and the crisis simultaneously, with the same unbroken line. Combining two distinct lines —a horizontal one of continuity and a vertical one of crisis—into one figure does not do justice to the insistence of the New Testament upon the inseparability of crisis and continuity. How can one line symbolize them both at the same time? There are two figures that can symbolize crisis and continuity simultaneously, the parabola and the spiral. Origen and Irenaeus draw these two figures for the shape of death.

This is not to disparage Cyprian's triangle of mortality, rich in pastoral wisdom and Christian discernment. In an eloquent statement of what several of his interpreters have called his Christian Stoicism, Cyprian urges his readers:

Beloved brethren, with sound mind, with firm faith, with rugged virtue, let us be ready for every manifestation of God's will; freed from the terror of death, let us think of the immortality that follows. Let us show that this is what we believe, so that we may not mourn the death even of our dear ones and, when the day of our own summons comes, without hesitation but with gladness we may come to the Lord at His call.

THE PARABOLA OF ETERNITY

IV

THE PARABOLA OF ETERNITY

DEATH is man's fate, but it need not be his ultimate destiny. In this conviction Christian faith and Platonic philosophy agree. Behind and beyond "all the changes and chances of this mortal life" both faith and philosophy envision an ultimate reality that abides, a reality in which mortal men may participate and thus live forever. The vision of that ultimate reality beyond existence and beyond death enables men to live out this mortal life with courage and hope. But how does it affect their attitude toward temporal, earthly existence? Tatian is proof that a refusal to speculate about what may lie behind and beyond existence can give to existence the quality of seriousness and decisiveness. Clement of Alexandria illustrates the danger that pre-occupation with what lies behind and beyond this mortal life may eventually shrivel existence into a mere episode within the great cosmic cycle of the soul.

Clement's determination to resist this danger leaves unsolved the problem of harmonizing the shape of death and the picture of eternity. It remains for Clement's illustrious successor and pupil, Origen, to try to draw a picture of eternity in which all shapes, including the shape of death, stand in proper perspective. How can a man earnestly contemplate the shape of death and yet escape the tyranny of death? How can a man raise his vision to eternity and still pay responsible attention to the unrepeatable and crucial decisions of life and of death? Origen, whose vision is on eternity, still takes these decisions with utmost seriousness. "Death," he says, "becomes precious for us, if we are saints of God, and if we are not unworthy to die." The vision of eternity makes sainthood in this present life important; being "not unworthy to die" means recognizing this present life, the arc of existence, as a decisive part of the parabola of eternity.

To the task of drawing this parabola Origen brings a preparation and an ability almost unmatched in the history of Christian thought. As Father Daniélou summarizes in the conclusion of his masterful book on Origen:

Francois Mauriac once said of Pascal: "Every kind of greatness met in one man, and that man was a Christian." Now that we have finished our study of Origen, we can say the same of him too. He is of that rare class of men whose genius is equalled only by their sanctity. . . . That is the way of it with really great men: they are equally good at all the possible ways of being great.

This combination of genius and sanctity determines Origen's conception of the role of the theologian. His sanctity prompts him to hear and obey the voice of God as it speaks in the Scriptures. It moves him also to heed the voice of the church as it defines its faith and doctrine. He is, in the phrase of another interpreter, "a man of the church." Where Scripture has not spoken and the church has not defined, however, there the genius of Origen feels authorized to ponder and to speculate. "The supreme function of knowledge," he writes in his commentary on the Song of Songs, "is to know the Trinity; and, in the second place, to know God's creation." When he launches into some of his speculations about the shape of death, he makes it clear that these questions have not been "distinguished with sufficient clearness in the teaching of the church." Since they have not, Christian believers may—and indeed Christian intellectuals must—examine the various answers to them and try to find one that is consistent with both divine revelation and the best achievements of the human mind.

For Origen, it is clear, the best achievements of the

79

human mind are the philosophical ideas of the Greeks, particularly those of Middle Platonism. "Do not suppose," he warns his readers, "that it is not consistent with Christian doctrine when in my reply to Celsus I accepted the opinions of those philosophers who have affirmed the immortality or the survival of the soul. We have some ideas in common with them." A little earlier in the treatise against Celsus he declares his intention "to state the proof for the doctrine of immortality, not only on the ground of what has been well said by the Greeks on this subject, but also in accordance with the divine teachings." The careful historical research of the last two or three decades has made it possible to identify more precisely the Greeks upon whom Origen draws for his philosophical ideas about the origin and destiny of the soul. Instead of speaking loosely about Plato or about Neoplatonism, historians of thought now label as "Middle Platonism" the species of Platonic thinkers to whom Origen is most directly indebted for his thought about the soul and about the shape of death. On the fact of Origen's debt to Middle Platonism interpreters of Origen are quite well agreed.

They are not as well agreed on the extent of Origen's debt to Middle Platonism. The very problem of the shape of death is the one most directly at issue; for, as was said earlier, Christianity has no doctrine of the soul. This means that Christian theologians must look beyond Scripture and tradition for the content of their ideas about the soul and about the shape of death. It does not mean that Christian theologians may use that content indiscriminately or that the selection of these extra-Biblical sources is a matter of indifference. When Origen speaks of the soul and of the shape of death as he does, has he been sufficiently discriminating in his use of extra-Biblical sources, or has he capitulated to Middle Platonism? Is his extensive and often extravagant use of allegorical interpretation a way of supplying biblical authority to support his non-Biblical or even anti-Biblical teaching about the parabola of eternity? Some interpreters affirm this and represent Origen as a speculative genius who occasionally pays his respects to the church but the rest of the time goes his own way. Others emphasize Origen's devotion to Scripture and tradition so exclusively as to give the impression that philosophy is unimportant to him. Most scholars acknowledge the biblical source of many of Origen's doctrines at the same time that they seek to track down the philosophical source of other doctrines, and in all his doctrines they recognize the subtle influence of each source upon the other.

Origen is a philosopher in spite of himself, but even as a philosopher he is a son of the church and an interpreter of the Sacred Scriptures. Failure to discern the faithfulness to Scripture and tradition that underlay even his philosophical speculations has prompted lesser men of later generations to brand him a heretic—even though in doing so they have had to use terms and concepts inherited from him. Although in the strict formal sense he personally does not seem to have been declared a heretic, some of his ideas were declared heretical at

81

the Second Council of Constantinople in A.D. 553. The ideas that were condemned were the same bold conceptions that formed the parabola of eternity, namely, the pre-existence of souls and the ultimate restoration of all things to unity in God. "Whoever says or thinks," declare the "anathematisms" of the Emperor Justinian, "that human souls pre-existed, *i.e.*, that they had previously been spirits and holy powers, but that, satiated with the vision of God, they turned to evil, and in this way the divine love in them died out and they therefore became souls and had been condemned to punishment in bodies, shall be anathema." Concerning the other arm of the parabola, the anathemas declare: "If anyone should say that the life of the spirits is to resemble the life that was in the beginning when the spirits had not yet come down or fallen, so that the end and the beginning are to be alike, and that the end is to be the true measure of the beginning: let him be anathema." Nevertheless, Origen's parabola of eternity forms one of the most creative attempts in Christian history to fit the arc of existence and the shape of death into the sweep of God's eternal, cosmic time.

The two arms of the parabola are the pre-existence of souls, which includes their prehistorical fall, and the eventual restoration of all things, which Origen, following the language if not perhaps the thought of the New Testament, calls the "apocatastasis." The pre-existence of souls, as Origen develops it, is one of the three possible explanations that he enumerates for the origin of the human soul. The three explanations are:

THE PARABOLA OF ETERNITY

creationism, that a soul is specially created and is introduced into the body when the body is being formed; traducianism, that the soul, like the body, is transmitted from one generation to the next in a natural manner; and pre-existence, that the soul antedates the body and comes into the body at the appropriate moment. Finding no set explanation in the teaching of the church, Origen believes himself free to choose from among these alternative theories. He summarizes these theories more than once in his writings. The most familiar summary appears in the first book of his great treatise *On First Principles*. Another, which occurs in his commentary on the Song of Songs, is less familiar and a trifle less controversial; for the treatise *On First Principles* has suffered both from the compulsive orthodoxy of Rufinus, who translated it into Latin, and from the heresy hunting of later theologians.

The soul ought to know, writes Origen in his commentary,

how she is constituted in herself, whether her being is corporeal or incorporeal, and whether it is simple, or consists of two or three or several elements; also, as some would enquire, whether the substance of the soul has been made, or has definitely not been made by anyone; and if it has been made, how it was made; whether, as some opine, its substance is contained in the bodily seed and originates together with the first beginning of the body; or whether it is introduced from the outside into the womb of a woman, and there united, as a perfect thing, to the body already

83

prepared and formed for it. And, if this be the case, whether it comes as a new creation that has only just been made when the body is seen to have been formed; in which case we should adjudge the reason for its creation to be the need for furnishing the body with a soul; or whether we should think that, having been created some time earlier, it comes for some reason to assume a body. And, if it is believed to be thus drawn into the body for some cause, then the work of knowledge is to determine what that cause may be.

Every indication points to the conclusion that Origen holds to this last theory, namely, that the soul, "having been created some time earlier, comes for some reason to assume a body." Although Origen's own writings have been badly bowdlerized, we have enough evidence to support this conclusion. In fact, it seems to be a quotation from the unexpurgated edition of Origen when Gregory of Nyssa says: "I have heard people maintain that the life of the soul did not begin when the soul was joined to the body; there were souls alive, they say, and grouped in nations in a world of their own before that. . . . Yielding to a sort of inclination towards evil, they lose their wings and come to have bodies." Created as spirits, they cool in their ardor for God and fall into the condition of being souls. Later they are punished still more by being bound to bodies in the empirical world. From the high point of their beginning in God, these rational creatures descend along the parabolic orbit and eventually come into the arc of existence as human individuals, furnished with bodies and set apart both from one another and from unity with God.

In this way the left side of the parabola of eternity is formed. It begins in God and before history, then leads downward into history. But it does not stop there. The right half of the parabola is like the left, leading through history, beyond history, and back to God. The souls, as Gregory of Nyssa continues in his summary of Origenism, "afterwards return by the same stages and are restored to the heavenly regions. . . . There is thus a kind of cycle, perpetually passing through the same stages; the soul never settles in any one state for ever." The biblical support for this speculation about the ultimate return and restoration of the soul comes not only from the biblical word "apocatastasis," but even more from the text that forms the keystone of Origen's eschatology (as well as of his Christology), I Cor. 15:25-28: "He [Christ] must reign until he has put all his enemies under his feet. The last enemy to be destroyed is death. . . . When all things are subjected to him, then the Son himself will also be subjected to him who put all things under him, that God may be all in all." Interpreting these words in the light of his theory of pre-existence, Origen completes his picture of the shape of death by drawing the right half of the parabola.

So then, when the end has been restored to the beginning, and the termination of things compared with their commencement, that condition of things will be re-established in which rational nature was placed, when it had no need to eat of the tree of knowledge of good and evil; so that when all feeling of wickedness has been removed, and the individual has been purified and cleansed, He who alone is the one good God becomes to him "all," and that not in the case of a few individuals, or of a considerable number, but He Himself is "all in all." And when death shall no longer anywhere exist, nor the sting of death, nor any evil at all, then verily God will be "all in all."

Origen cannot be persuaded that God has truly become "all in all" or "everything to every one" so long as death remains. Giving death the last word would be a negation of God. To describe the shape of death in true perspective, therefore, the line of the figure must extend beyond an existence where death does have the last word. The line must go on beyond death and beyond history, back into the One and the All, "who alone is the one good God."

So the parabola is complete. Between birth and death the parabola passes through the arc of existence, when the soul is joined to the body and leads an individual, historical existence. In fact, it is the very character of that existence that compels Origen to extrapolate this brief span into something older and longer. His vision of a cosmos reunited with God, who is "all in all," has room for the conversion of even the devil; for giving the devil the last word would likewise be a negation of God. If this is truly man's origin and if such is really man's destiny, what happens to the decisiveness of historical existence? Is Heinrich Karpp correct, for example, when he maintains that by drawing the parabola of eternity Origen "makes all earthly life a mere episode in the life of the soul, or more precisely, of the spirits"? Theologian and philosopher that he is, Origen is not unaware of this very danger. His figure for the shape of death should be called "the parabola of eternity" rather than "the circle of immortality" because his chief endeavor is to set his speculation apart from those doctrines of eternity and immortality which do make the arc of existence "a mere episode in the life of the soul."

One such doctrine is a strict metaphysical dualism, which teaches that the antithesis between the material and the spiritual is eternal. Preoccupied though he is with this antithesis, Origen refuses to make it eternal; for this would be tantamount to a denial of God the Creator. Although he teaches the pre-existence of souls, this must not be permitted to violate the biblical teaching

that the universe was created by God and that there is no substance that has not received its existence from Him. This refutes and dismisses the doctrines falsely taught by some, that there is a matter that is co-eternal with God, or that there are unbegotten souls, in whom they would have it that God implanted not so much the principle of existence as the quality and rank of their life.

Thus he will not take the easy way to an explanation of the relation between the eternal life of the soul and its temporal existence in the body. For the soul too is a creature, and so is matter; the conflict between them has been going on for a long time, but there was a time when souls were not and hence when there was no conflict.

Nor will he follow the related path of absolute idealism, the identification of matter and the body with evil as such. There are certainly many passages in his writings that indicate some such identification. He can say, in commenting upon the biblical injunction to love God with the "whole soul":

> I believe that they love God with their "whole" soul who, because of their great desire to be united with Him, separate and cut off their soul not only from the earthly body but from every kind of body. Without distraction or disturbance they undergo separation from "the body of their lowliness" when through death, as it is held to be, the opportunity offers of putting away "the body of this death."

This seems to put Origen unambiguously into the tradition of a Christianized Neoplatonism or Platonized Christianity. When he is more careful and precise, however, he makes it clear that this idealistic explanation will not do either. The polemics of Celsus compels such precision and care. "What is properly speaking abominable," he writes against Celsus, "is of the nature of evil. But the nature of the body is not abominable; for in itself bodily nature is not involved in evil, which is the originating cause of what is abominable." And again a little later: "In our view it is not true that 'the matter that dwells among mortals' is responsible for evils. Each person's mind is responsible for the evil that exists in him, and this is what evil is. Evils are the actions that result from it. In our view nothing else is strictly speaking evil." Though he may speak in Neoplatonic fashion and call the body a prison for the soul, thus disparaging the arc of existence, he knows better when he thinks about it. He realizes that he cannot make this an explanation for the shape of death and the parabola of eternity.

The form of the parabola likewise prohibits Origen from accepting the circle as an explanation for the shape of death, time, and eternity. He distinguishes among the various proponents of this explanation. "The Stoics," he finds, "maintain that the universe periodically undergoes a conflagration and after that a restoration of order in which everything is indistinguishable from what happened in the previous restoration of the world." "The Pythagoreans and Platonists," on the other hand, teach that "when in certain fixed cycles the stars adopt the same configuration and relationships to each other . . . everything on earth is in the same position as it was at the last time when the relationship of the stars in the universe to one another was the same." With both these explanations he contrasts the doctrine of "us who say that the universe is cared for by God in accordance with the conditions of the free will of each man, and that as far as possible it is always being led on to be better, . . . and that the nature of our free will is to admit various possibilities." If the cycle theory were true, one would have to say that "Jesus will again come to visit this life and will do the same things that he has done, not just once but an infinite number of times according to the cycles." The course of human history under the providence of God must have motion and direction because of the unrepeatable coming of Jesus Christ. A circle makes such motion and direction an illusion, and therefore Origen cannot adopt this shape as an explanation for the pilgrimage of the soul from eternity through time and death and back to eternity.

For many of the same reasons Origen cannot adopt the cognate theory of the transmigration of souls. It seems to be almost a necessary corollary to the doctrine of pre-existence, and Origen apparently considers it worth discussing

whether the soul puts on a body only once and, having laid it down, seeks for it no more; or whether, when it once has laid aside what it took, it takes it yet again; and, if it does so a second time, whether it keeps what it has taken always, or some day puts it off once more. But if, as the Scriptures lead us to think, the consummation of the world is near and this present state of corruption will be changed into one of incorruption, there seems no doubt that the soul cannot come to the body a second or third time under the conditions of this present life. For, if this other view were accepted, then the world would know no end of such successive re-assumptions.

Significantly, it is the biblical idea of the consummation of history that clinches Origen's case against transmigration. If history is moving toward a goal, there must be something decisive about the actions and experiences of the soul within the arc of existence. The arc must be part of a larger shape, but that shape dare not be so closed and self-contained that the soul's movement toward its goal becomes meaningless.

Because Origen is not simply a philosopher, despite his philosophical propensities, but a man of the church and an expositor of the Scriptures, these philosophical arguments for pre-existence and restoration prove unacceptable to him. Neither dualism nor idealism can finally explain the conflict between flesh and spirit; neither the cycle theory of history nor the theory of transmigration can satisfactorily account for the movement of the soul through time and death to God. To support his doctrines of pre-existence and restoration Origen must turn to other considerations than these. He must find grounds for his doctrines either in the direct assertions of the Scriptures or—since the Scriptures are silent on these issues—in speculations that are in harmony with the assertions of the Scriptures and perhaps even derivable from them.

One such assertion is the biblical doctrine of creation,

that God, the Creator of all things, is good, and just, and all-powerful. When He in the beginning created those beings which He desired to create, i.e., rational natures, He had no other reason for creating them than on account of Himself, i.e., His own goodness. As He Himself, then, was the cause of the existence of those things which were to be created, in whom there was neither any variation nor change, nor want of power, He created all whom He made equal and alike, because there was in Himself no reason for producing variety and diversity.

From this interpretation of creation it necessarily follows that "the cause of the diversity among rational creatures [is] not from the will or judgment of the Creator, but from the freedom of the individual will." That much Origen says in the expurgated text of *On First Principles* translated by Rufinus, but a Greek fragment of the same book is more explicit in stating the case for pre-existence on the basis of the contrast between the essential unity of creation and the diversity of historical existence:

Before the aeons existed, all spirits were pure; demons, souls, and angels alike, all served God and did what He commanded them. The devil was one of them. He had free will and wanted to set himself up against God, but God cast him down. All the other powers fell with him. The biggest sinners became demons, lesser ones became angels, the least archangels. Thus the portions allotted depended on the sins of the recipients. Other souls were not sinful enough to be made demons but were too sinful to be made angels. These God punished by making the world, binding them to bodies and putting them into it. Although these spiritual creatures, then, all had the same nature, God made some of them demons, some angels, and some men. That does not mean that He is a respecter of persons. No, what He did was in keeping with their sins. If it were not so, and if the soul had no previous existence, how is it that we find men blind from birth, before they could possibly have sinned, and why do others go blind though they have done nothing wrong?

Not the eternal circle of being, but the act of God in creating, requires that the diversity within historical existence be explained by reference to a previous state of the soul. The doctrine of creation seems to imply something like the downward path on the left side of the parabola.

The doctrine of redemption, on the other hand, seems to imply something like the upward path on the right side of the parabola. In the history of the doctrine of redemption Origen is usually remembered for his somewhat bizarre suggestion that the humanity of Christ is like bait on the hook of his divinity, to catch the devil by tricking him. Origen is remembered also for his statements that the Son of God is inferior to the Father. Both these positions take the place they do in Origen because Christ is the first to describe the parabola of eternity in his own life and work. Origen argues for the parabola, i.e., for pre-existence and restoration, on the basis of Christ. He writes:

If Celsus had understood what is appropriate for a soul that will have everlasting life, and what is the right view of its essence and origin, he would not have ridiculed in this way the idea of an immortal person entering a mortal body. Our view here does not accept the Platonic doctrine of the transmigration of souls, but a different and more sublime view.

93

"The idea of an immortal person entering a mortal body" is the doctrine of the incarnation, as Origen understands it and as Celsus misunderstands it. This doctrine is incomprehensible to Celsus because he does not grasp "what is appropriate for a soul that will have everlasting life, and what is the right view of its essence and origin." That is, Celsus sees neither the right half of the parabola, the life eternal that awaits the soul, nor the left half of the parabola, the essence and origin of the soul in creation and pre-existence. The parabolic path of incarnation and return to glory, described by the life of Jesus Christ, becomes paradigmatic for the parabola of eternity now being described by the life of the soul.

What applies to Christ completely, applies to the soul in part. "These words [of praise for her beauty] are spoken by the Word of God to the soul that has indeed been set in the path of progress, but has not yet attained the summit of perfection. She is called beautiful because she is advancing." The advance of the soul through time and death to the perfection of eternity requires that the shape of death be something like a parabola. Origen's philosophical inclinations make the notion of an endless succession of worlds attractive to him, but his Christianity teaches him that there is an "end" toward which history moves. Even the present corrupt text of *On First Principles* shows the conflict in his mind between these two world views, and in some Greek fragments the inclination toward a doctrine of endless succession is even more pronounced. Yet it would be a mistake to see in pre-existence and restoration nothing but concessions by Origen the exegete to Origen the philosopher. It is Origen the exegete who is convinced that in God's providence the soul "as far as possible is always being led on to be better," and this conviction forces him to conclude that the soul had an existence before its existence in the body. A similar premise leads Clement of Alexandria to another conclusion: "The soul is certainly not sent down from heaven into some worse condition. For God is working everything up to some better condition." Progress under divine providence proves to Clement that the soul has no pre-existence; to Origen it proves the opposite.

The progress of the soul from pre-existence through birth to existence, and then from existence through death to eternity, culminates in "apocatastasis," when the primal condition is restored in God. Reflecting on this restoration, Origen writes: "Let us, I say, from such an end as this, contemplate the beginnings of things. For the end is always like the beginning; and, therefore, as there is one end to all things, so ought we to understand that there was one beginning." In a similar vein he argues that the soul could not become like the angels unless it had been so originally. "For one would think it possible for that which has been lost to be restored, but not for that to be bestowed which the Creator did not give in the beginning." End and beginning must somehow match. Yet for this, too, Origenism was condemned, for teaching that "the end and the beginning are to be alike, and that the end is to be the true measure of the beginning." Taken as it stands, such a view of time and history seems to be nothing more than the cyclical theory. After descending from its original state, the soul describes a circular path until it returns to exactly the same place where it originally began.

Origen knows, however, that the Christian hope for the life eternal is not identical with this cyclical theory. He contrasts the two very explicitly:

> We hold that, as from the grain of corn an ear rises up, so in the body there lies a certain principle that is not corrupted, from which the body is raised in incorruption. But it is the Stoics who say that after the body has been entirely corrupted it will return to its original nature, because they believe in the doctrine that each world-period is indistinguishable; and it is they who say that it will again be composed in the same first condition that it had before it was dissolved, proving this, as they imagine, on the ground of logical necessities.

This is, to be sure, written about the body rather than about the soul; but behind it lies a Christian understanding of linear time that breaks with the theory of endlessly recurring cycles. Yet the end is like the beginning: as the soul takes its origin from God, so it envisions its destiny in God. It moves from eternity to eternity, but it moves through time and existence and death. Death is inevitable, but the shape of death now fits into the parabola of eternity. Because he sees the arc of existence as a decisive part of this parabola of eternity, Origen can raise his vision to eternity and still pay responsible attention to the unrepeatable and crucial decisions of life and of death. He can earnestly contemplate the shape of death, but because of Christ he can escape the tyranny of death. As theological theories, pre-existence and restoration are both highly suspect, and the church knew what it was doing when it condemned them. But the vision of life, death, and eternity under God that produces these theories is the vision by which the church lives in wonder and devotion even when it condemns the theories.

Contemplating this vision of the parabola of eternity as the shape of death, Origen expresses his wonder and his devotion:

Is it possible that all this should happen to each one of us and that even the last enemy, death, should be destroyed, so that Christ may say in us: "O death, where is thy sting? O Hades, where is thy victory?" Let then "what is corruptible" in us "put on" holiness and "incorruption" in chastity and all purity, and "what is mortal," having conquered death, "put on the immortality" of the Father. Thus God will be reigning in us, and we shall already enjoy the benefits of regeneration and resurrection.

THE SPIRAL OF HISTORY

V

THE SPIRAL OF HISTORY

I N the midst of life we are in death," for death is the
end of life. Yet in the midst of death we are in life,
for life is the end of death. Because both these declara-
tions are true, the shape of life and of death cannot be
represented by a circle; for a circle has neither end nor
motion, and life does move toward an end in death. It
cannot be a straight line either, for each man who lives
and dies represents and repeats the recurring pattern of
the human race. Nowhere is a man more alone than
when he dies, yet nowhere does he have more in com-

101

mon with all men. The death of a man is unique, and yet it is universal. The straight line would symbolize its uniqueness, the circle its universality. But how can one figure symbolize both?

Christianity declares that in the life and death of Jesus Christ the unique and the universal concur. Perhaps no church father saw this concurrence of the unique and the universal as clearly, or formulated it as precisely, as Irenaeus. To be the Savior and the Lord, Jesus Christ has to be a historical individual with a biography all his own; he dare not be a cosmic aeon that swoops to earth for a while but never identifies itself with man's history. Yet this utterly individual historical person must also contain within himself the common history of mankind. His history is his alone, yet each man must recognize his own history in it. His death is his alone, yet each man can see his own death in the crucifixion of Jesus. Each man can identify himself with the history and the death of Jesus Christ because Jesus Christ has identified himself with human history and human death, coming as the head of a new humanity. Not a circle, then, nor a straight line, but a spiral represents the shape of death as Irenaeus sees it; for a spiral has motion as well as recurrence. As represented by a spiral, history may, in some sense, be said to repeat itself; yet each historical event remains unique. Christ is both unique and universal.

The first turn of the spiral is the primeval history of humanity in Adam. As Origen interprets the end of history on the basis of its beginning, so Irenaeus portrays the story of Adam on the basis of the story of Christ. "Whence, then, comes the substance of the first man? From God's Will and Wisdom, and from virgin earth. For 'God had not rained,' says the Scripture, before man was made, 'and there was no man to till the earth.' From this earth, then, while it was still virgin God took dust and fashioned the man, the beginning of humanity." Irenaeus does not regard Adam and Eve merely as private individuals, but as universal human beings, who were and are all of humanity. Adam and Eve were perfect, not in the sense that they possessed perfection, but in the sense that they were capable of development toward perfection. They were, in fact, children. Irenaeus does not claim pre-existence for the human soul; therefore there is no need for him, as there is for Origen, to identify existence itself with the fall. Existence is created and willed by God and is not the consequence of a pre-existent rebellion or of a cosmic descent from eternity into history. Historical existence is a created good.

The biblical symbol for this affirmation is expressed in the words: "So God created man in his own image; in the similitude of God he created him." There are some passages in the writings of Irenaeus where the image of God and the similitude are sharply distinguished, so most notably in the statement: "If the [Holy] Spirit is absent from the soul, such a man is indeed of an animal nature; and, being left carnal, he will be an imperfect being, possessing the image [of God] in his formation, but not receiving the similitude [of God]

103

through the Spirit." Thus the image of God is that which makes a man a man and not an oyster; the similitude of God, by contrast, is that which makes a man a child of God and not merely a rational creature. Recent research on Irenaeus, however, makes it evident that he does not consistently maintain this distinction. He does not mean to say that Adam lost the similitude of God and his immortality through the fall; for he was created not exactly immortal, nor yet exactly mortal, but capable of immortality as well as of mortality.

Therefore Irenaeus describes man's creation as follows:

So that the man should not have thoughts of grandeur, and become lifted up, as if he had no lord, because of the dominion that had been given to him, and the freedom, fall into sin against God his Creator, overstepping his bounds, and take up an attitude of self-conceited arrogance towards God, a law was given him by God, that he might know that he had for lord the lord of all. And He laid down for him certain conditions: so that, if he kept the command of God, then he would always remain as he was, that is, immortal; but if he did not, he would become mortal, melting into earth, whence his frame had been taken.

These conditions man did not keep, and thus he became mortal; yet he did not stop being human as a result. There is no justification for systematizing the random statements of Irenaeus about the image of God beyond this, nor for reading into his imprecise usage the later theological distinction between the image of

God (humanity) and the similitude of God (immortality).

Man was created with the capacity for immortality, but the devil's promise of immortality in exchange for disobedience cost Adam his immortality. He was, in the words of Irenaeus, "beguiled by another under the pretext of immortality." The true way to immortality lay through obedience, but man did not believe this.

Eve was disobedient; for she did not obey when as yet she was a virgin. And even as she, having indeed a husband, Adam, but being nevertheless as yet a virgin . . . , having become disobedient, was made the cause of death, both to herself and to the entire human race; so also did Mary, having a man betrothed [to her], and being nevertheless a virgin, by yielding obedience, become the cause of salvation, both to herself and the whole human race.

Because he interprets the primitive state of man as one of mere potentiality or capacity and believes that Adam and Eve were created as children, Irenaeus often seems inclined to extenuate their disobedience as being "due, no doubt, to carelessness, but still wicked." His interpretation of the beginning on the basis of the end prompts him to draw these parallels between the Virgin Eve and the Virgin Mary. That parallelism affects his picture of man's disobedience too; for as it was Christ, the Word of God, who came to rescue man, so it was disobedience to the word of God in the beginning that brought death into the world, and all our woe.

With this act of disobedience, and not with the in-

ception of his individual existence, man began the downward circuit on the spiral of history, descending from
the created capacity for immortality to an inescapable
mortality. At the nadir of that circuit is death. "Along
with the fruit they did also fall under the power of
death, because they did eat in disobedience; and disobedience to God entails death. Wherefore, as they
became forfeit to death, from that [moment] they were
handed over to it." This leads Irenaeus to the somewhat startling notion that Adam and Eve died on the
same day that they disobeyed, namely, on a Friday, as a
parallel to the death of Christ on Good Friday; he sees
a parallel also to the Jewish day of preparation for the
Sabbath. In any case, though they had been promised
immortality if they ate of the tree, they obtained mortality instead. The wages of sin is death. Man's life,
originally shaped for immortality and for communion
with God, must now be conformed to the shape of
death.

Nevertheless, even at the nadir of the circuit the
spiral of history belongs to God, and he still rules. Even
death, therefore, has a providential as well as a punitive
function.

Wherefore also He [God] drove him [man] out of Para-
dise, and removed him far from the tree of life, not because
He envied him the tree of life, as some venture to assert,
but because He pitied him, [and did not desire] that he
should continue a sinner for ever, nor that the sin which
surrounded him should be immortal, and evil interminable

and irremediable. But He set a bound to his [state of] sin, by interposing death, and thus causing sin to cease, putting an end to it by the dissolution of the flesh, which should take place in the earth, so that man, ceasing at length to live in sin, and dying to it, might live to God.

This idea, which occurs in both Tatian and Cyprian, fits especially well into the scheme of Irenaeus' theology; for it prepares the way for the passage from life through death to life that is achieved in Christ. As man can live only by dying, so it was only by his dying that Christ could bring many to life.

It is probably fair to say that the idea of death is more profound in Irenaeus than the idea of sin is. This applies to his picture of Adam. It is borne out also by the absence of any developed theory about how sin passes from one generation to the next. It becomes most evident in his description of Christ as the second Adam, who does indeed come to destroy sin, but whose work culminates in the achievement of immortality. This emphasis upon death rather than sin as man's fundamental problem Irenaeus shares with many early theologians, especially the Greek-speaking ones. They speak of the work of Christ as the bestowal of incorruptibility, which can mean (though it does not have to mean) deliverance from time and history.

Death reminds man of his sin, but it reminds him also of his transience. It represents a punishment that he knows he deserves, but it also symbolizes most dramatically that he lives his life within the process of time. These

107

two aspects of death cannot be successfully separated, but they dare not be confused or identified. The repeated efforts in Christian history to describe death as altogether the consequence of human sin show that these two aspects of death cannot be separated. Such efforts almost always find themselves compelled to ask whether Adam was created capable of growing old and then older and then still older, in short, whether Adam's life was intended to be part of the process of time. If it was, then it must have been God's intention to translate him at a certain point from time to eternity. One night, so some of these theories run, Adam would have fallen asleep, much as he fell asleep for the creation of Eve; and thus he would have been carried over into the life eternal. The embarrassment of these theories over the naturalness of death is an illustration of the thesis that death cannot be only a punishment, for some termination seems necessary in a life that is lived within the natural order of time and change.

On the other hand, Christian faith knows that death is more than the natural termination of temporal existence. It is the wages of sin, and its sting is the law. If this aspect of death as punishment is not distinguished from the idea of death as natural termination, the conclusion seems inevitable that temporal existence itself is a form of punishment rather than the state into which man is put by the will of the Creator. This seems to have been the conclusion to which Origen was forced. If death receives more than its share of attention from the theologian and if sin receives less than its share, the gift of the life eternal through Christ begins to look like the divinely appointed means of rescue from temporal, i.e., created, existence. Such an interpretation of death radically alters the Christian view of creation; for it teaches salvation from, not salvation in, time and history. Because Christianity teaches not only salvation in history, but salvation by the history of Christ, such an interpretation of death would require a drastic revision of the Christian understanding of the work of Christ.

The most characteristic term for Irenaeus' understanding of the work of Christ is "recapitulation." Because the spiral of history is the shape of death, recapitulation means that history takes a new turn with the coming of Christ, but that the new turn follows the pattern of the old turn. It is a new turn, for "he brought all [possible] novelty, by bringing himself who had been announced. For this very thing was proclaimed before hand, that a novelty should come to renew and quicken mankind. . . . But when the King has actually come . . . , the question will not be then asked by any that are possessed of sense what new thing the King has brought." The great novelty of his coming is his personal presence as the Jesus Christ of history. This is completely new, and yet it is the recapitulation of something very old. Therefore,

just as it was through a virgin who disobeyed that man was stricken and fell and died, so too it was through the Virgin, who obeyed the word of God, that man resuscitated by life

109

received life. For the Lord came to seek back the lost sheep, and it was man who was lost; and therefore he did not become some other formation, but he likewise, of her that was descended from Adam, preserved the likeness of formation; for Adam had necessarily to be restored in Christ, that mortality be absorbed in immortality, and Eve in Mary, that a virgin, become the advocate of a virgin, should undo and destroy virginal disobedience by virginal obedience.

The curve of the incarnation thus repeats the pattern of the creation, so that what was lost after the fall from the original creation might be recovered the next time around. The spiral of history moves into a new stage that surrounds and thus repeats the old; but when it does, it shows that God patterned the old turn after that which was to come. Now man can show that he has the image of God, and now he can regain the lost similitude of God.

This Word was manifested when the Word of God was made man, assimilating himself to man, and man to himself, so that by means of his resemblance to the Son, man might become precious to the Father. For in times long past, it was said that man was created after the image of God, but it was not yet [actually] shown; for the Word was as yet invisible, after whose image man was created. Wherefore also he did easily lose the similitude. When, however, the Word of God became flesh, he confirmed both these; for he both showed forth the image truly, since he became himself what was the image; and he re-established the

110

similitude after a sure manner, by assimilating man to the invisible Father through the means of the visible Word.

The downward plunge of the curve of Adam takes place when Adam disobeys the word and command of God. When Christ follows this path, his obedience must make up for the primal disobedience. This begins when the Virgin Mary obeys the word of God and thus undoes the damage caused by the disobedience of the Virgin Eve. Christ carries out this obedience at every stage of his life. He "passed through every stage of life, restoring to all communion with God." Earlier Irenaeus says:

Being a master, [Christ] also possessed the age of a master, not despising or evading any condition of humanity, nor setting aside in himself that law which he had appointed for the human race, but sanctifying every age, by that period corresponding to it which belonged to himself. . . . He therefore passed through every age, becoming an infant for infants . . . a child for children . . . a youth for youths. So likewise he was an old man for old men.

Thus it is that the sins of disobedience at each point along the spiral curve now meet their master, as he follows the curve and lives through all the ages of man in obedience to the law of the Father.

At just this point, however, it is important to remember that Irenaeus has a more profound concept of death than of sin. This applies also to his picture of Christ. Although he sets forth his theory of a reconciliation by

111

installments, which requires that he make Christ an old man to atone for old men, he is interested most in the points at the two termini of the arc of existence—the birth of Christ and the death of Christ. Therefore he says: "He sanctified our birth and abolished death." And again:

Doing away with [the effects of] that disobedience of man which had taken place at the beginning by the occasion of a tree, "he became obedient unto death, even the death of the cross." . . . In the second Adam, however, we are reconciled, being made obedient even unto death. For we were debtors to none other but to Him whose commandment we had transgressed at the beginning.

As death is the true shape of life and the nadir of the curve for Adam and for humanity in Adam, so Christ comes to die. He describes the entire orbit of human life, from birth to death, in order to reconcile the whole of life to God.

Christ lives in the shape of death because that is the shape of human life. As his life comes full circle in its imitation of the pattern set by the life of humanity in Adam, he comes to the death of the cross. Irenaeus has no explicit theory how the death of Christ accomplishes the reconciliation between God and man; but he does have many images and metaphors, apparently taken over from the liturgical and exegetical tradition of his time. He does know as a certainty that as death is the nadir of man's life, so it must be the nadir of Christ's life.

Because, being all implicated in the first formation of Adam, we were bound to death through disobedience, the bonds of death had necessarily to be loosed through the obedience of him who was made man for us; because death ruled in the body, it was necessarily through the body that it should be done away with and man go free from its oppression. So "the Word was made flesh," in order that sin, destroyed by means of that same flesh through which it had gained the mastery and taken hold and lorded it, should no longer be in us; and therefore the Lord took up the same first formation for an incarnation, that so he might join battle on behalf of his forefathers, and overcome through Adam what had stricken us through Adam.

So far, then, the curve of Christ's life is a repetition of the curve of man's life in Adam. Both begin in God, both end in death; between birth and death Christ is obedient where man is disobedient, but this does not excuse him from death. Yet Irenaeus is drawing the shape of death as a spiral of history to show that through Christ the dreary old curve of human life takes a new turn. The line goes all the way down to the nadir of death, but it goes through death and begins to curve upward again. About the resurrection as about the crucifixion of Christ Irenaeus has no consistent or worked-out theory, but he does attach importance to it in the scheme of salvation. "By dying and rising again," he writes, Christ "was to be permanently immortal. . . . What, then, is the point of [the words] 'he sought life,' since he was to die? He [the prophet in Ps. 20] is therefore proclaiming his resurrection from

113

the dead, and that having risen from the dead, he is immortal; for he received 'life' that he might rise again, and 'length of days for ever and ever,' that he might be incorruptible." Having taken on flesh, Christ is obedient to the death of the cross. To live a genuine human life means to live a life that is formed by the shape of death. By going through death rather than around death, he transforms the shape of death into the shape of life. As a result of the first curve of the spiral it is necessary to say: "In the midst of life we are in death." But as a result of this second curve of the spiral it is possible to say: "In the midst of death we are in life."

This is what makes the coming of Christ literally a matter of life and death. His history must be as genuine a part of the human story as the history of Adam or the history of any other man. Irenaeus defends the genuineness of this history with all the passion and rhetoric he can summon against the heretics who transform the story of Christ into something less than history in their effort to transform it into something more than history. Only if his history is a real history can it save men who live and die in real history. There must be continuity between the history of man and the history of Christ; otherwise all life is ultimately conformed to the shape of death, and the nadir of death is the end of history, for Christ and for all men. "If he was not [truly] born, neither did he die; and if he did not die, neither was he raised from the dead; and if he was not raised from the dead, he has not conquered death, nor is its reign abolished; and if death is not conquered, how are we to

114

mount on high into life, being subject from the beginning to death?" The curve of Christ's life takes on the shape of death and follows the curve of humanity in Adam, so that the spiral of history may go beyond the nadir of death and so that the curve of man's life may follow the curve of Christ's life through death to the new life in God.

Therefore:

Now God shall be glorified in His handiwork, fitting it so as to be conformable to, and modelled after, His own Son . . . . Those, then, are the perfect who have had the Spirit of God remaining in them, and have preserved their souls and bodies blameless, holding fast the faith of God, that is, that faith which is [directed] toward God, and maintaining righteous dealings with respect to their neighbors.

Irenaeus describes the curve of life once in his description of humanity in Adam, a second time and at great length in his description of humanity in Christ, and a third time, though briefly, in his references to this new humanity as it manifests itself in the new life of believers in Christ. Quoting the words, "As we have borne the image of him who is of the earth, we shall also bear the image of him who is from heaven," Irenaeus exhorts his readers: "As therefore, when we were destitute of the celestial Spirit, we walked in former times in the oldness of the flesh, not obeying God; so now let us, receiving the Spirit, walk in newness of life, obeying God." Because in Christ life takes a new turn, there can be a new life, a renewed image of God, a new obedi-

115

ence, and victory over death. The spiral of history can describe the pattern set not by Adam but by Christ, the shape of life and not the shape of death.

This means that the similitude of God, lost in Adam and present in Christ, may now be present in man as well. Christ is the new pattern for the spiral, encircling all that Adam is, but adding to it and renewing it. "When he became incarnate, and was made man, he commenced afresh the long line of human beings, and furnished it, in a brief, comprehensive manner, with salvation; so that what we had lost in Adam—namely, to be according to the image and likeness of God—that we might recover in Christ Jesus." Irenaeus is so vivid in his description of this new curve of the spiral that he can speak of Christ's becoming man in order that man might become God. Sometimes, as Lawson points out, Irenaeus speaks of "this process of divinization . . . almost in mechanical terms, as though it were a sort of spiritual inoculation." In the main, however, this criticism does not hold, partly because the chief object of attention in Irenaeus' doctrine of Christ, and therefore in his doctrine of the new man in Christ, is neither sin and its forgiveness nor yet divinization, but the shape of death and the achievement of immortality. Salvation is the gift of immortality from God. If death is the shape of life on account of the disobedience of Adam, life may now become the final shape of death on account of the obedience of Christ—this declaration describes the new curve of the spiral.

Irenaeus summarizes:

116

As, then, he who was made a living soul forfeited life when he turned aside to what was evil, so, on the other hand, the same individual, when he reverts to what is good, and receives the quickening Spirit, shall find life. . . . This same [total man, body, soul and spirit] therefore, was what the Lord came to quicken, that as in Adam we do all die, as being of an animal nature, in Christ we may all live, as being spiritual.

In another passage Irenaeus summarizes all three curves in the spiral of history that is the true shape of death—the curve of Adam, the curve of Christ, and the curve of the new humanity in Christ. To draw the shape of death means to trace the entire spiral. It begins with Adam; and, continually moving around its axis it also continually recedes from Adam to Christ and describes a pattern that is old and yet new, unique and yet universal.

"The law," he writes, "did truly take away death's kingdom, showing that he was no king, but a robber; and it revealed him as a murderer." Thus the law of God showed that the life of man was not intended to be conformed to the shape of death, but had been created for life. At the same time the law "laid a weighty burden upon man, who had sin in himself, showing that he was liable to death." Because of this liability, man had to conform to the shape of death even while he knew that he had been made for something better. He had to walk the treadmill of life and follow the pattern of Adam, conscious all along that this should not be the

117

direction of his life. Therefore "it behooved him who was
to destroy sin, and redeem man under the power of
death, that he should himself be made the very same
thing which he was, that is, man." Christ came into the
form of a servant and into the shape of death, and fol-
lowed the curved pattern established by Adam,

who had been drawn by sin into bondage, but was held by
death, so that sin should be destroyed by man, and man
should go forth from death. For as by the disobedience of
the one man who was originally moulded from virgin soil,
the many were made sinners, and forfeited life; so it was
necessary that, by the obedience of one man, who was originally born from a virgin, many should be justified and receive salvation.

So in Christ life can come full circle. As he descends
to the nadir of human existence and takes on the shape
of death, man may ascend to the zenith of Christ's existence and even take on the shape of life. The pattern
of life and death as described by Irenaeus has both end
and motion, yet it recognizes that each man who lives
and dies represents and repeats the recurring pattern
of the human race. The spiral of history includes both
the nadirs and the zeniths, both the beginning and the
end, both the unique and the universal. "Whether,
therefore, we live or die, we are the Lord's."

CONCLUSION

THE core of the Christian faith is pessimism about life and optimism about God and therefore hope for life in God. The ground for the pessimism, the optimism, and the hope is the church's recollection and celebration of the life, death, and resurrection of her Lord. This survey of the images in which five church fathers sketch the shape of death compels the question: What, then, is the true shape of death? Other questions can wait, if need be forever. But this question affects every man personally, and it may become crucial for

any man at any moment. Each of these five geometric
figures says something important about the shape of
death. The arc of existence emphasizes the finality of
death. The circle of immortality represents the analogy
between the life of man and the eternal life of God. The
triangle of mortality says that even with an immortal
soul a man must die to God and receive life from God.
The parabola of eternity makes death God's way of
bringing the soul back to himself. The spiral of history
urges that the death of a man cannot be understood apart
from the death of Adam and the death of Christ.

Is there any figure that can say all of this at once, and
say it better? There is, but it is not technically a geometric figure. It is the figure of the cross. Signed with
the cross at baptism, the believer is signed with it again
at death; thus it symbolizes the arc of existence. The
cross is the disclosure of something mysterious in the
very heart of God, his capacity to know the meaning
of human suffering and death; thus—like the circle of
immortality, but far more profoundly—the cross describes the analogy between the life of man and the eternal life of God. The cross marks the death of One who
lived completely for God and who died in unbroken
unity with God, who therefore received life from God
and was raised from the dead to the glory of God the
Father; thus it brings together, more radically than the
triangle of mortality can, the horizontal and the vertical
lines in the shape of death. On the cross hangs the figure
of him "who for us men and for our salvation came down
from heaven and was incarnate by the Holy Ghost of

the Virgin Mary and was made man," but who, having been raised again according to the Scriptures, has received a kingdom that has no end; thus it defines the lowest point, and at the same time it delineates both the origin and the destiny, of the parabola of eternity. Yet the figure on the cross is the second Adam, who went into the Garden of Gethsemane to save those who had been expelled from the Garden of Eden, that "he who by a tree once overcame might likewise by a tree be overcome, through Christ our Lord"; thus the spiral of history is fulfilled and drawn clearly for all to see and, seeing, to believe.

The cross leaves many questions unanswered, much of death uncharted. Men have pondered the mystery of their own death and wondered about the unknown. All the clinical information about death at our disposal only makes this mystery more profound and this wonder more haunting. The Christian view of death is not intended to supplement this clinical information with additional data about the human constitution. It is intended to give men the faith to live in courage and to die in dignity, knowing very little about the undiscovered country except that, by the grace of his cross, our Lord Jesus Christ has changed the shape of death. That is all we can know, that is all we need to know.

BIBLIOGRAPHY

Almost all the direct quotations in this book can be found in the various English editions of the fathers. Most of them, however, have been checked and corrected on the basis of the original Greek and Latin, or newly translated by the present author. The major exception to this is, of course, the *Epideixis* or *Proof of the Apostolic Preaching* by Irenaeus, which is available in an Armenian version and in two English translations based upon that, but in neither Greek nor Latin manuscripts.

Atzberger, L. *Geschichte der christlichen Eschatologie*. Freiburg, 1896.

Bonwetsch, G. N. *Die Theologie des Irenaeus*. Gütersloh, 1925.

Chadwick, H. "Origen, Celsus, and the Resurrection of the Body," *Harvard Theological Review*, XLI (1948), 83-102.

Cochrane, Charles Norris. *Christianity and Classical Culture*. New York, 1944.

Cullmann, Oscar. *Immortality of the Soul or Resurrection of the Dead?* New York, 1958.

Daniélou, Jean. *Origen*. Translated by Walter Mitchell. New York, 1955.

Dinkler, Erich. *Die Anthropologie Augustins*. Stuttgart, 1934.

Elze, Martin. *Tatian und Seine Theologie*. Göttingen, 1960.

Favez, Charles. *La consolation latine chrétienne*. Paris, 1937.

Geffcken, J. *Zwei griechische Apologeten*. Leipzig, 1907.

Gerhardt, M. *Die Bedeutung der Eschatologie bei Irenäus*. Berlin, 1922.

Grant, Robert. "The Resurrection of the Body," *The Journal of Religion*, XXVII (1948), 120-30, 188-208.

Hanson, R. P. C. *Origen's Doctrine of Tradition*. London, 1954.

Hering, Jean. *Étude sur la doctrine de la chute et de la pré-existence des âmes chez Clément d' Alexandrie*. Paris, 1923.

Karpp, Heinrich. *Probleme altchristlicher Anthropologie*. Gütersloh, 1950.

Koch, Hal. *Pronoia und Paideusis*. Berlin, 1932.

————. *Virgo Eva—Virgo Maria*. Berlin, 1937.

Lawson, John. *The Biblical Theology of Saint Irenaeus*. London, 1948.

Lubac, Henri de. *Histoire et esprit*. Paris, 1950.

Pelikan, Jaroslav, "The Eschatology of Tertullian," *Church History*, XXI (1952), 108-22.

Puech, A. *Recherches sur le Discours aux Grecs de Tatien*. Paris, 1903.

Rohde, E. *Psyche*. Translated by W. Hillis. London, 1925.

Rush, Alfred. *Death and Burial in Christian Antiquity*. Washington, 1941.

Scharl, E. *Recapitulatio mundi*. Freiburg, 1941.

Wingren, Gustaf. *Man and the Incarnation*. Translated by Ross Mackenzie. Philadelphia, 1959.

Witt, R. E. *Albinus and the History of Middle Platonism*. Cambridge, 1937.

INDEX